Dessert Cakes

Dessert Cakes

Delectable ways to finish a meal with 50 recipes for every occasion

ANN NICOL

southwater

This edition is published by Southwater,
an imprint of Anness Publishing Ltd,
Blaby Road, Wigston, Leicestershire LE18 4SE

info@anness.com

www.southwaterbooks.com; www.annesspublishing.com

If you like the images in this book and would like to investigate using
them for publishing, promotions or advertising, please visit our
website www.practicalpictures.com for more information.

Publisher: Joanna Lorenz
Editorial Director: Helen Sudell
Editors: Kate Eddison and Simona Hill
Photographer: William Lingwood
Stylist: Liz Hippisley
Home Economist: Lucy McKelvie
Designer: Nigel Partridge
Production Controller: Pirong Wang

PUBLISHER'S NOTE
Although the advice and information in this book are believed to be
accurate and true at the time of going to press, neither the authors
nor the publisher can accept any legal responsibility or liability for
any errors or omissions that may have been made nor for any
inaccuracies nor for any loss, harm or injury that comes about from
following instructions or advice in this book.

NOTES
• Bracketed terms are intended for American readers.
• For all recipes, quantities are given in both metric and imperial
measures and, where appropriate, in standard cups and spoons.
Follow one set of measures, but not a mixture, because they are
not interchangeable.
• Standard spoon and cup measures are level. 1 tsp = 5ml,
1 tbsp = 15ml, 1 cup = 250ml/8fl oz.
• Australian standard tablespoons are 20ml. Australian readers should
use 3 tsp in place of 1 tbsp for measuring small quantities.
• American pints are 16fl oz/2 cups. American readers should use
20fl oz/2.5 cups in place of 1 pint when measuring liquids.
• Electric oven temperatures in this book are for conventional ovens.
When using a fan oven, the temperature will probably need to be
reduced by about 10–20°C/20–40°F. Since ovens vary, check with
your manufacturer's instruction book for guidance.
• The nutritional analysis given for each recipe is calculated per
portion (i.e. serving or item), unless otherwise stated. If the recipe
gives a range, such as Serves 4–6, then the nutritional analysis will be
for the smaller portion size, i.e. 6 servings. The analysis does not
include optional ingredients, such as salt added to taste.
• Medium (US large) eggs are used unless stated.
• Recipes containing raw eggs should not be eaten by pregnant
women, babies, the very young and elderly people. You can use dried
egg whites instead which give excellent results and can be substituted
in recipes.

Main front cover image shows Cinnamon apple gâteau – for recipe,
see pages 44–5

Previously published as part of a larger volume, *The Best-Ever Book
of Cakes*.

Contents

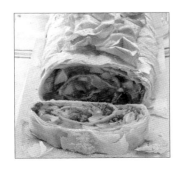

Introduction

For those who love to bake, both young and old, this is the perfect compendium of dessert cakes. Traditional tried-and-tested cake recipes sit alongside moreish contemporary creations that can be served at any time of day, as well as a heavenly treat to end the meal with.

Baking produces so much pleasure. There's a real sense of achievement when you create a fresh batch of delicious cakes, and the whole house is filled with the marvellous aroma of baking. Home-made cakes must be the most popular, homely food you could make, and old favourites are always welcomed, but it's also fun to try something new. You'll find an almost overwhelming choice here. Each chapter deals with a different group of cakes, from sweet and sticky cakes and gâteaux, meringues and pastries to indulgent chocolate cakes and iced cakes, cheesecakes and showstoppers.

BAKING SKILLS

If you are a less experienced baker, remember that there are no secrets to making a cake; just follow the simple methods to ensure successful results. Baking and cake-making involve several different techniques, and some cakes will certainly require more skill than others, but as you bake the recipes that appeal to you, you'll gradually build up your confidence and expertise. Step-by-step photographs guide you through each stage, showing how the ingredients should look at specific points of making.

IN THIS BOOK

The recipes included here are made with a wide range of methods and for different skill levels. There are cakes of every kind here, so there is sure to be something that will appeal to all ages and palates. You'll find fruity cakes, nutty cakes, and rich and gooey chocolate cakes, as well as stunning creations for those extra special occasions. Some are quick and easy to make with minimal ingredients, whereas others require a little more time. The Sweet and Sticky Cakes chapter includes both delicious and flavourful fresh fruit treats as well as dried fruit and spice combinations. These cakes may well include your favourite flavouring ingredients: try Apple Cake, Poppy Seed Cake, or Date and Walnut Spice Cake for everyday eating.

For special gatherings the Gâteaux, Meringues and Pastries chapter provides the perfect serving suggestions. These cakes can be simple to make, as with Sponge Cake with Strawberries and Cream, or divine creations upon which you can lavish time and attention, such as Cinnamon Meringues or Chocolate and Strawberry-filled Palmiers. Chocolate must be the most popular ingredient in baking, and the Indulgent Chocolate Cakes chapter offers a superb selection of delectable treats. Black Forest Gâteau, Frosted Chocolate Fudge Cake and Sachertorte are just a few of the classics featured.

The final chapter, Iced Cakes, Cheesecakes and Showstoppers, include recipes that require a little extra preparation. A special cake brings a personal touch and can be made as a gift or a stunning centrepiece. There is an iced pavlova, a fruity mousse cake, mouthwatering cheesecakes, as well as an impressive tower of choux buns filled with cream, and a heavenly meringue mountain to be made. Whatever your skill level, taste preferences and occasion, the ideal recipe will be included in the following pages.

Left Everyone loves a chocolate cake and this versatile ingredient complements so many other flavours.

Right This sophisticated-looking cake is a sponge covered in vanilla custard cream and tinted almond marzipan.

Fillings and toppings

Cakes are made extra special by adding a filling or topping, and there are many different coverings to suit a variety of uses. Use sugarpaste icing on celebration cakes, or frostings on gâteaux, or decorate with simple frosted flowers.

Buttercream icing

This rich icing makes a good cake covering and filling, or can be used to adhere sugarpaste icing to cakes.

MAKES 350G/12OZ/2 CUPS

75g/3oz/6 tbsp unsalted
  butter, softened
225g/8oz/2 cups icing
  (confectioners') sugar, sifted
5ml/1 tsp vanilla extract
10ml/2 tsp milk

1 Place the butter, icing sugar and vanilla extract in a bowl and whisk or beat with a wooden spoon.

2 Add the milk and beat until soft, smooth and fluffy. Store, chilled, for up to 2 days in a covered container.

BUTTERCREAM VARIATIONS
• Coffee: Blend 10ml/2 tsp coffee essence with the milk and omit the vanilla extract.
• Citrus: Omit the vanilla extract and milk, add 30ml/2 tbsp orange or lemon juice and the finely grated zest of half the fruit.

Ganache

This rich icing makes a perfect topping or filling for a rich chocolate cake for a special occasion.

MAKES 350G/12OZ/2 CUPS

250ml/8fl oz/1 cup double
  (heavy) cream
225g/8oz plain (semisweet)
  chocolate, broken into pieces

Gently heat both ingredients in a pan, stirring until melted. Pour into a bowl, leave to cool, then spread over the the cake.

Vanilla frosting

Use this smooth and creamy frosting as a filling and topping.

MAKES 150G/5OZ/SCANT 1 CUP

150g/5oz/generous 1 cup icing
  (confectioners') sugar
25ml/5 tsp vegetable oil
15ml/1 tbsp milk
a few drops of vanilla extract

Sift the icing sugar into a bowl and beat in the oil, milk and vanilla extract until smooth and creamy.

Chocolate fudge frosting

Rich and tasty, this glossy frosting can be poured over a cake or spread as a filling and topping.

MAKES 350G/12OZ/2 CUPS

115g/4oz plain (semisweet)
  chocolate, broken into pieces
50g/2oz/½ cup unsalted butter
1 egg, beaten
175g/6oz/1½ cups icing
  (confectioners') sugar, sifted
2.5ml/½ tsp vanilla extract

1 Melt the chocolate and butter in a bowl set over a pan of hot water.

2 Remove from the heat and whisk in the egg, icing sugar and vanilla. Whisk until smooth. Use at once or leave to cool and thicken.

Glacé icing

Because it is made to a pourable consistency, this icing is used to drizzle over sponge cakes.

MAKES 225G/8OZ/1½ CUPS

225g/8oz/2 cups icing
 (confectioners') sugar
a few drops of vanilla extract
30–45ml/2–3 tbsp hot water
food colouring (optional)

1 Sift the icing sugar into a bowl and add flavouring. Gradually add enough water to mix to a consistency of thick cream.

2 Beat with a wooden spoon until the icing is thick enough to coat the back of the spoon. Add colouring, if you like, and use at once, as the icing will begin to form a skin. Liquid food colourings are ideal.

GLACÉ ICING VARIATIONS
• Citrus: Replace the water with freshly squeezed, strained orange or lemon juice.
• Chocolate: Sift 10ml/2 tsp unsweetened cocoa powder into the icing (confectioners') sugar.
• Coffee: Dissolve 5ml/1 tsp coffee granules in 15ml/1 tbsp of hot water, then cool, or add 5ml/1 tsp liquid coffee extract.

Making a paper piping (pastry) bag

Paper piping bags are useful for piping with or without a nozzle.

1 Cut out a 38 × 25cm/15 × 10in rectangle of baking parchment. Fold it diagonally in half to form two triangles. Cut along the fold line.

2 The long edge of the triangle forms the top opening edge of the piping bag. Roll one short side of the triangle into the centre to make a sharp-pointed cone, and hold in place at the centre. Fold the other end around the cone.

3 Hold all the points together at the back of the cone, keeping the pointed end sharp. Fold the outer layer firmly inside the top edge to lock in place. Keep the layers of the bag together. If they start to separate the bag will lose its strength and the icing forced through the tip may rip the bag. Snip a tiny hole at the tip. Part-fill with icing. Fold over the top.

Crystallized decorations

Flowers, berries, petals and leaves can all be crystallized and make a perfect addition to special cakes.

1 Wash herb sprigs, leaves or edible berries, under gently running water, then pat dry with kitchen paper. Leave to dry.

2 Separate petals from rosebuds, and brush small flowers such as violets or primroses using a clean paintbrush, but do not wash them.

3 Beat 1 egg white with 15ml/1 tbsp cold water until frothy.

4 Liberally paint the herbs, leaves, berries or petals with the egg white on all sides.

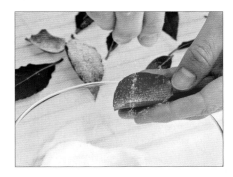

5 Sprinkle the painted items lightly with caster (superfine) sugar while still damp, and shake off any excess. Leave to dry on waxed paper in a warm place. Attach them to the cake with royal icing.

Apricot glaze

Use apricot glaze for sticking almond paste to a cake or for adding a shiny finish to toppings.

MAKES 450G/1LB/2 CUPS

450g/1lb/1 cup apricot jam
5ml/1 tsp lemon juice

1 Put the ingredients in a pan with 45ml/3 tbsp water. Heat gently, stir until melted. Boil fast for 1 minute.

2 Press through a fine sieve (strainer).

3 Pour into a clean jar and store in the refrigerator for up to 3 months.

Almond paste

Marzipan protects and seals the cake and helps to fill any imperfections. It makes a flat area for icing.

MAKES 450G/1LB/2 CUPS

115g/4oz/1 cup sifted icing (confectioners') sugar
115g/4oz/generous ½ cup caster (superfine) sugar
225g/8oz/2 cups ground almonds
1 egg
5ml/1 tsp lemon juice
15ml/1 tbsp brandy

1 Stir the sugars and ground almonds together.

2 Whisk the egg, lemon juice and brandy together and mix into the dry ingredients.

3 Knead the almond paste until it is smooth. Pat into shape. Wrap the paste in clear film (plastic wrap) and store in the refrigerator for a maximum of 3 days.

To use almond paste

1 Knead the paste on a surface lightly dusted with icing (confectioners') sugar until soft. If the paste has been refrigerated, bring it back to room temperature first.

2 Place the cake upside down on a cake board so that the top is level.

3 Measure the circumference of the cake using a piece of string.

4 Brush the cake all over with apricot glaze. Fill in the gaps around the base with a rope of almond paste. Fill any holes or surface dips with small pieces of paste.

5 Roll out the almond paste to a square or circle large enough to cover the top of the cake. Make sure the paste is evenly rolled. Cut out the circle or square, then press it on top of the cake.

6 Roll a sausage of almond paste the length of the string, then use a rolling pin to roll it deep enough to cover the sides of the cake. Trim the edges. Roll it into a coil.

7 Roll the coiled strip around the side of the cake and press it on with the palms of your hands. Trim if necessary, and leave to dry out for at least 24 hours.

Royal icing
Use royal icing to cover Christmas or wedding cakes to form a snowy-white surface.

MAKES 500G/1¼LB

2 medium egg whites
500g/1¼lb/5 cups icing
 (confectioners') sugar, sifted
10ml/2 tsp lemon juice

1 Put the egg whites into a clean, grease-free bowl and whisk lightly with a fork to break up the whites until foamy.

2 Sift in half the icing sugar with the lemon juice, and beat well with a wooden spoon for 10 minutes, or until smooth.

3 Gradually sift in the remaining icing sugar and beat again until thick, smooth and brilliant white. Alternatively, use a hand-held electric mixer set on a slow speed to make the mixing easier.

4 Keep the royal icing covered with a damp cloth until you are ready to use it, or store in the refrigerator in a tightly lidded plastic container until needed. If making royal icing ahead of time for use later, beat it again before use to expel any air bubbles that may have formed in the mixture.

5 To cover a cake, spread the icing over the top and sides of the cake using a palette knife or metal spatula, then smooth down over the sides or flick into points with a knife to make a snowy effect. Leave the icing to dry and become firm for 3 days.

COOK'S TIP
For a softer royal icing that will not set too hard, beat 5ml/1 tsp of glycerine into the mixture. Glycerine is sold bottled in liquid form in pharmacies and larger supermarkets.

Dessert sauces

From classic custard to light fruit coulis, a sauce can instantly transform a simple cake to a delectable dessert for any season. Some are very quick and easy, others take a little effort – but the results will be well worth it, and are sure to impress any dinner guests.

Crème Anglaise

Here is the classic English custard – far superior to packet versions. It can turn a basic sponge into a warming winter pudding, or can act as an elegant cold sauce for fruity summer cakes. Delicious whether served hot or cold.

SERVES 4

1 vanilla pod (bean)
450ml/¾ pint/1⅞ cups full-fat (whole) milk
40g/1½oz/3 tbsp caster (superfine) sugar
4 egg yolks

1 Split the vanilla pod down the middle with a sharp knife and place in a pan with the milk. Bring slowly to the boil.

2 Remove the pan from the heat, then cover and leave to infuse for about 10 minutes, before removing and discarding the vanilla pod.

3 Beat together the caster sugar and egg yolks until the mixture is thick, light and creamy.

4 Slowly pour the warm milk on to the egg mixture, stirring constantly.

5 Place the bowl over a pan of hot water. Stir constantly over a low heat for 10 minutes, or until it coats the back of the spoon. Remove from the heat immediately to prevent curdling.

6 Strain and serve immediately. If serving cold, strain and cover the surface with baking parchment.

Glossy Chocolate Sauce

Delicious poured over chocolate cakes, this sauce also freezes well.

SERVES 6

115g/4oz/½ cup caster (superfine) sugar
175g/6oz plain (semisweet) chocolate, broken into squares
30ml/2 tbsp unsalted butter
30ml/2 tbsp brandy or orange juice

1 Place the sugar and 60ml/4 tbsp of water in a pan. Heat gently, stirring occasionally, until the sugar dissolves.

2 Stir in the chocolate, a few squares at a time, until melted, then add the butter in the same way. Do not allow the sauce to boil. Stir in the brandy or orange juice and serve warm.

Chocolate Fudge Sauce

This is a real treat if you're not counting calories. Serve it with a simple chocolate cake, and add some scoops of good quality vanilla ice cream, for a special touch.

SERVES 6

150ml/¼ pint/⅔ cup double (heavy) cream
50g/2oz/4 tbsp butter
50g/2oz/¼ cup granulated (white) sugar
175g/6oz plain (semisweet) chocolate
30ml/2 tbsp brandy

1 Heat the double cream with the butter and sugar in the top of a double boiler or in a heatproof bowl set over a pan of hot (not boiling) water. Stir until smooth.

2 Break the plain chocolate into pieces, and add to the cream mixture. Stir until it is melted and thoroughly combined.

3 Stir in the brandy a little at a time, then allow the chocolate fudge sauce to cool to room temperature before serving.

CHOCOLATE FUDGE SAUCE VARIATIONS

These delectable variations on the classic chocolate fudge sauce are great to have up your sleeve. They are perfect when used to match either a citrus- or coffee-based dessert cake respectively.
• White Chocolate and Orange: replace the granulated (white) sugar with 40g/1½ oz/3 tbsp caster (superfine) sugar, the plain (semisweet) chocolate with white chocolate and the brandy with orange liqueur, and add the finely grated rind of 1 orange. Add the orange rind in step 1 with the cream, butter and sugar, and follow the recipe to the end using the substituted ingredients.
• Coffee and Chocolate: Replace the granulated (white) sugar with soft light brown sugar and the brandy with coffee liqueur or dark rum, and add 15ml/1 tbsp coffee extract. Follow the recipe instructions, using the substituted ingredients, and add the coffee extract at the end.

Raspberry Coulis

This is a simple way to turn a quick cake into an impressive dessert.

1 Purée raspberries, with icing (confectioners') sugar to taste, then press through a sieve (strainer).

2 Blend a little cornflour (cornstarch) with some orange juice, and stir into the purée. Cook for 2 minutes in a pan over a medium heat, stirring, until thick. Allow to cool.

Black Forest Sauce

This sauce adds a new dimension to a classic chocolate cake.

1 Drain a can of black cherries, reserving the juice. Blend a little of the juice with a little cornflour (cornstarch).

2 Add the cornflour mixture to the rest of the juice in a pan. Heat, stirring, until boiling and slightly thickened, then add the cherries and a dash of Kirsch and heat through.

Sweet and Sticky Cakes

Cakes made using luscious fresh fruits can often double up
as a pudding, but it is best that these are eaten on the day
of baking, as the pieces of fruit will eventually soften.
Apple Cake and Pear and Polenta Cake ooze with juicy
fruits and are delicious eaten warm, whereas delicate
Greek Yogurt and Fig Cake or Gooseberry Cake are
wonderful chilled, served with lashings of cream.

Gooseberry cake

Gooseberries can be slightly acidic, so here they are sweetened with sugar and elderflower 30 minutes before they are added to the cake batter. The elderflower infuses the batter with a light, sweet flavour. Serve this fresh as a pudding with a spoonful of crème fraîche.

SERVES 10

75g/3oz/6 tbsp butter, melted,
   plus extra for greasing
150g/5oz gooseberries
22.5ml/4½ tsp golden caster
   (superfine) sugar
15ml/1 tbsp elderflower cordial,
   plus extra for brushing
225g/8oz/2 cups plain
   (all-purpose) flour
10ml/2 tsp baking powder
150g/5oz/¾ cup golden caster
   (superfine) sugar
2.5ml/½ tsp vanilla extract
1 egg, lightly beaten
250ml/8fl oz/1 cup buttermilk
icing (confectioners') sugar,
   for dusting

1 Preheat the oven to 180°C/ 350°F/Gas 4. Grease a 23cm/9in round loose-based cake tin (pan) with butter.

2 Arrange the fruit in a single layer on a plate and sprinkle evenly with the sugar and elderflower cordial. Leave to stand for 30 minutes.

3 Sift the dry ingredients into a large bowl and make a well in the centre.

4 In a separate bowl, lightly whisk together the melted butter, vanilla extract, egg and buttermilk. Pour into the dry ingredients and fold partly together.

5 Lightly combine half the reserved gooseberries and all of the syrupy juices into the batter, then fold together with a metal spoon.

6 Spoon the mixture into the tin and sprinkle the remaining fruit on top.

7 Bake for 30 minutes, but check after 25 minutes. If the centre of the cake is springy to the touch, it is ready. Lightly brush the surface of the warm cake with elderflower cordial, if you like, and serve, dusted with icing sugar.

Energy 273kcal/1144kJ; Protein 3.9g; Carbohydrate 34.6g, of which sugars 18.1g; Fat 14.2g, of which saturates 8.3g; Cholesterol 82mg; Calcium 51mg; Fibre 1g; Sodium 112mg.

Greek yogurt and fig cake

Fresh figs, thickly sliced then baked in honey, make a delectable base that becomes a topping for a featherlight sponge. Figs that are a little on the firm side work best for this particular recipe. Keep refrigerated in an airtight container for two days.

SERVES 8–10

200g/7oz/scant 1 cup butter,
  softened, plus extra for greasing
6 firm fresh figs, thickly sliced
45ml/3 tbsp clear honey, plus extra
  for glazing
175g/6oz/scant 1 cup caster
  (superfine) sugar
grated rind of 1 lemon
grated rind of 1 orange
4 eggs, separated
225g/8oz/2 cups plain
  (all-purpose) flour
5ml/1 tsp baking powder
5ml/1 tsp bicarbonate of soda
  (baking soda)
250ml/8fl oz/1 cup Greek
  (US strained plain) yogurt

1 Preheat the oven to 180C/350°F/ Gas 4. Grease and line the base of a 23cm/9in cake tin (pan) with baking parchment.

2 Arrange the sliced figs over the base of the tin and drizzle over the honey.

3 In a large bowl, beat the butter and sugar together with the citrus rinds until pale and fluffy.

4 Gradually beat in the egg yolks.

5 Sift the dry ingredients into the creamed mixture in batches, alternating with a spoonful of yogurt. Beat well, then repeat this process until all the dry ingredients and yogurt have been incorporated.

6 Put the egg whites into a clean, grease-free bowl and whisk until they form stiff peaks.

7 Stir the egg whites into the cake batter in two batches. Pour the mixture over the figs in the tin and smooth the top level. Bake for 1¼ hours, or until golden and a skewer inserted into the centre of the cake comes out clean.

8 Turn the cake out on to a wire rack, peel off the lining paper and cool. Drizzle the fig topping with extra honey before serving.

Energy 473kcal/1982kJ; Protein 8.2g; Carbohydrate 59.5g, of which sugars 38g; Fat 24.3g, of which saturates 14g; Cholesterol 149mg; Calcium 167mg; Fibre 2g; Sodium 225mg.

Pear and polenta cake

This light polenta sponge has a nutty corn flavour that complements the fruit perfectly. For this upside-down cake, pears and honey are added to the base of the cake tin, then the mixture is added on top. Serve as a dessert with custard or whipped cream, if you like. Eat fresh.

3 Cut the pears into chunky slices and toss them in the lemon juice.

4 Arrange the pears on the base of the cake tin. Drizzle the honey over, and set aside.

SERVES 10

butter, for greasing
175g/6oz/scant 1 cup golden caster (superfine) sugar
4 ripe pears, peeled and cored
juice of ½ lemon
30ml/2 tbsp clear honey
3 eggs
seeds from 1 vanilla pod (bean)
120ml/4fl oz/½ cup sunflower oil
115g/4oz/1 cup self-raising (self-rising) flour
50g/2oz/⅓ cup instant polenta (cornmeal)

1 Preheat the oven to 180°C/350°F/Gas 4. Grease and line a 20cm/8in round cake tin (pan) with baking parchment.

2 Sprinkle 30ml/2 tbsp of the sugar over the base of the prepared tin.

COOK'S TIP
To release the seeds from the vanilla pod, cut down the centre with a sharp knife, then scoop out the seeds with a teaspoon.

5 In a bowl, mix together the eggs, the seeds from the vanilla pod and the remaining sugar. Beat until thick and creamy, then gradually beat in the oil.

6 Sift the flour and polenta into the egg mixture and fold in. Pour the batter over the pears in the tin.

7 Bake for 50 minutes, or until a skewer inserted into the centre comes out clean. Cool in the tin for 10 minutes, then turn the cake out, and peel off the lining paper.

Energy 256kcal/1077kJ; Protein 3.7g; Carbohydrate 38.9g, of which sugars 26.7g; Fat 10.5g, of which saturates 1.5g; Cholesterol 57mg; Calcium 65mg; Fibre 1.8g; Sodium 66mg.

Yogurt cake with pistachio nuts

Flavoured with vanilla seeds and pistachio nuts, this unusual cake contains very little flour. The texture is lightened with whisked egg whites. Serve it with crème fraîche and passion fruit or summer berries to make a soft and sweet summer dessert. Eat fresh for the best taste.

SERVES 8–12

butter, for greasing
3 eggs, separated
75g/3oz/scant ½ cup caster
    (superfine) sugar
seeds from 2 vanilla pods (beans)
300ml/½ pint/1¼ cup Greek (US
    strained plain) yogurt
grated rind and juice of 1 lemon
15ml/1 tbsp plain
    (all-purpose) flour
handful of pistachio nuts,
    roughly chopped
90ml/6 tbsp crème fraîche, to serve
4–6 fresh passion fruit, or
    50g/2oz/½ cup summer berries,
    to serve

1 Preheat the oven to 180°C/350°F/
Gas 4. Grease and line a 25cm/10in
square shallow tin (pan) with
baking parchment.

2 In a mixing bowl, beat the egg
yolks with 50g/2oz/¼ cup sugar
until pale and fluffy.

3 Beat in the vanilla seeds and stir in
the yogurt, lemon rind and juice.
Sift in the flour and beat well until
light and airy.

4 Put the egg whites into a clean,
grease-free bowl and whisk until
they form stiff peaks, then gradually
whisk in the rest of the sugar to
form soft peaks.

5 Fold the whisked whites into the
yogurt mixture. Turn the batter into
the cake tin.

6 Put the tin in a roasting pan and
pour water in the pan to come
halfway up the cake tin. Bake for 20
minutes, or until risen and just set.

7 Sprinkle the nuts over the cake
and bake for another 20 minutes.
Serve warm or cold with crème
fraîche and a spoonful of fruit.

Energy 152kcal/638kJ; Protein 6.6g; Carbohydrate 16g, of which sugars 14.1g; Fat 7.9g, of which saturates 3.4g; Cholesterol 95mg; Calcium 99mg; Fibre 0.1g; Sodium 71mg.

Apple cake

This recipe comes from the West of England and uses cooking apples to give the cake a moist texture and a refreshing sweet-and-sour flavour. You can use eating apples, if you prefer, for a sweeter result. This is best eaten fresh with clotted cream or vanilla ice cream.

SERVES 8

115g/4oz/½ cup butter, diced,
   plus extra for greasing
225g/8oz cooking apples, peeled,
   cored and chopped
juice of ½ lemon
225g/8oz/2 cups plain
   (all-purpose) flour
7.5ml/1½ tsp baking powder
165g/5½oz/scant ¾ cup soft
   light brown sugar
1 egg, beaten
30–45ml/2–3 tbsp milk
2.5ml/½ tsp ground cinnamon

1 Preheat the oven to 180°C/ 350°F/Gas 4. Grease and line an 18cm/7in round cake tin (pan) with baking parchment.

2 In a small bowl, toss the apples with the lemon juice.

3 Sift the flour and baking powder into a large bowl.

4 With cold hands, rub the butter into the flour mixture until it resembles fine crumbs. Stir in 115g/4oz/½ cup of the sugar, and the apples.

5 Add the egg and enough milk to give a soft, dropping consistency.

6 Spoon into the prepared tin and smooth the top level.

7 Mix together the remaining sugar with the cinnamon, then sprinkle over the cake batter.

8 Bake for 45–50 minutes, or until firm to the touch. Leave to cool, then turn out on to a wire rack to go cold. Peel off the lining paper.

COOK'S TIP
Steps 3 and 4 can be made ahead of time and the dry crumbs stored in the refrigerator.

Energy 476kcal/2003kJ; Protein 4.5g; Carbohydrate 74.6g, of which sugars 56.5g; Fat 19.8g, of which saturates 8.5g; Cholesterol 32.5mg; Calcium 77.1mg; Fibre 2g; Sodium 104.8mg.

Farmhouse apple and sultana cake

This is a traditional, flavourful country cake made very simply and easily using the creaming method. It has a sweet, crispy top, a lovely moist texture and a spicy apple flavour – it makes a nice dessert served with custard or cream. Keep for two days in an airtight container in a cool place.

SERVES 12

175g/6oz/¾ cup softened butter, plus extra for greasing
175g/6oz/¾ cup soft light brown sugar
3 eggs
225g/8oz/2 cups self-raising (self-rising) flour, sifted
5ml/1 tsp baking powder, sifted
10ml/2 tsp mixed (apple pie) spice
350g/12oz cooking apples, peeled, cored and diced
175g/6oz/generous 1 cup sultanas (golden raisins)
75ml/5 tbsp milk
30ml/2 tbsp demerara (raw) sugar

1 Preheat the oven to 160°C/325°F/ Gas 3. Grease and line a 20cm/8in round deep cake tin (pan) with baking parchment.

2 Put the butter in a large bowl with the sugar. Beat together until light and fluffy. Beat in the eggs. Sift in the flour, baking powder and spice, then beat until thoroughly mixed.

3 Fold in the apples, sultanas and sufficient milk to make a soft dropping consistency.

4 Spoon the batter into the prepared tin. Wet a metal spoon by running it under the tap and use the back of the wet spoon to smooth the cake top level.

5 Sprinkle with demerara sugar. Bake for about 1½ hours, or until risen, golden brown and firm to the touch. Cool in the tin for 5 minutes, then turn out on to a wire rack.

Energy 310kcal/1305kJ; Protein 4.2g; Carbohydrate 45.5g, of which sugars 31.2g; Fat 13.7g, of which saturates 8.4g; Cholesterol 81mg; Calcium 63mg; Fibre 1.3g; Sodium 135mg.

Moist orange and almond cake

There are many techniques for adding moisture and flavour to cake batters. Here a whole orange is cooked slowly until completely tender and then blended to a purée. Ground almonds that add richness make the perfect partner. Eat fresh, served with orange slices and whipped cream.

SERVES 8

1 large orange, washed
butter, for greasing
3 eggs
225g/8oz/generous 1 cup caster
    (superfine) sugar
5ml/1 tsp baking powder
25g/1oz/¼ cup plain
    (all-purpose) flour
225g/8oz/2 cups ground almonds
icing (confectioners') sugar,
    for dusting
whipped cream and orange slices
    (optional), to serve

COOK'S TIP
For tender flesh, do not use a microwave to cook the orange.

1 Pierce the orange with a skewer. Put it in a deep pan and cover with water. Bring to the boil, lower the heat, cover and simmer for 1 hour, until soft. Drain, then cool.

2 Preheat the oven to 180°C/350°F/ Gas 4. Grease and line a 20cm/8in round deep cake tin (pan).

3 Cut the orange in half and discard the pips. Put the orange, skin and all, in a blender or food processor and purée until smooth and pulpy.

4 In a bowl, whisk the eggs and sugar. Fold in the baking powder, flour and almonds, then the purée.

5 Pour into the prepared tin, level the surface and bake for 1 hour, or until a skewer inserted into the middle comes out clean.

6 Allow to cool for 10 minutes, then turn out on to a wire rack to go cold. Peel off the lining paper.

7 Dust the cake with icing sugar and serve with whipped cream. Tuck thick orange slices under the cake just before serving, if you like.

Energy 187kcal/783kJ; Protein 5.1g; Carbohydrate 20g, of which sugars 18.2g; Fat 10.2g, of which saturates 1.1g; Cholesterol 41mg; Calcium 60mg; Fibre 1.4g; Sodium 19mg.

Crunchy-topped fresh apricot cake

Almonds are perfect partners for fresh apricots, and this is a great way to use fruits that may be a little too firm for eating. Chopped fresh nectarines make a good alternative when apricots are not available. Serve cold as a cake, or warm with custard for a dessert. It will keep for two days.

SERVES 8

175g/6oz/¾ cup butter, softened, plus extra for greasing
175g/6oz/1½ cups self-raising (self-rising) flour
175g/6oz/¾ cup caster (superfine) sugar
115g/4oz/1 cup ground almonds
3 eggs
5ml/1 tsp almond extract
2.5ml/½ tsp baking powder
8 firm apricots, stoned (pitted) and chopped

For the topping
30ml/2 tbsp demerara (raw) sugar
50g/2oz/½ cup flaked (sliced) almonds

1 Preheat the oven to 160°C/ 325°F/Gas 3. Grease and line an 18cm/7in round cake tin (pan) with baking parchment.

2 Put all the ingredients, except the apricots, in a large bowl or food processor and whisk or process until light and creamy.

3 Fold the apricots into the cake batter.

4 Spoon the cake batter into the prepared cake tin and smooth the top level. Make a hollow in the centre of the mixture with the back of a large spoon.

5 Sprinkle over 15ml/1 tbsp of the demerara sugar, then scatter the flaked almonds over the top.

6 Bake for 1½ hours, or until a skewer inserted into the centre comes out clean.

7 Sprinkle the remaining demerara sugar over the top of the cake and leave to cool for 10 minutes in the tin. Remove from the tin and peel off the paper. Finish cooling on a wire rack.

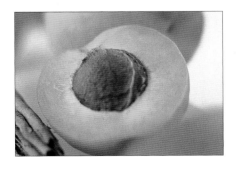

Energy 414kcal/1734kJ; Protein 6.2g; Carbohydrate 46.8g, of which sugars 30.3g; Fat 23.9g, of which saturates 12.3g; Cholesterol 118mg; Calcium 126mg; Fibre 1.8g; Sodium 241mg.

Lemon chiffon cake

Split a light lemon sponge cake in half horizontally, then fill with a lovely thick layer of lemon mousse to give it a tangy centre. Top with a lemon icing and lemon zest and you have the most lemony cake. Keep this for one day in the refrigerator, or freeze for two months, undecorated.

SERVES 8

butter, for greasing
2 eggs
75g/3oz/6 tbsp caster
 (superfine) sugar
grated rind of 1 lemon
50g/2oz/½ cup plain (all-purpose)
 flour, sifted
lemon shreds, to decorate

For the filling
2 eggs, separated
75g/3oz/6 tbsp caster
 (superfine) sugar
grated rind and juice of 1 lemon
15ml/1 tbsp gelatine
120ml/4fl oz/½ cup fromage frais
 or crème fraîche

For the icing
15ml/1 tbsp lemon juice
115g/4oz/1 cup icing
 (confectioners') sugar, sifted

1 Preheat the oven to 180°C/350°F/ Gas 4. Grease and line a 20cm/8in round loose-based cake tin (pan).

2 Whisk the eggs, sugar and lemon rind until mousse-like. Fold in the flour, then pour into the cake tin.

3 Bake for 20–25 minutes, or until the cake springs back when lightly pressed in the centre. Turn on to a rack to go cold. Clean the cake tin.

4 Remove the lining paper. Split the cake in half horizontally and return the lower half to the clean cake tin.

5 To make the filling, put the egg yolks, sugar, lemon rind and juice in a bowl. Beat with an electric whisk until thick, pale and creamy.

6 Pour 30ml/2 tbsp water into a small heatproof bowl and sprinkle the gelatine on top. Leave until spongy, then set the bowl over simmering water and stir until dissolved. Cool slightly, then whisk into the yolk mixture. Fold in the fromage frais or crème fraîche.

7 When the filling mixture begins to set, whisk the egg whites in a clean, grease-free bowl until they form soft peaks. Stir a spoonful into the mousse mixture to lighten it, then fold in the rest.

8 Pour the filling over the sponge in the cake tin, spreading it to the edges. Put the second layer of sponge on top and chill until set.

9 Slide a knife dipped in hot water between the tin and the cake to loosen it, then transfer the cake to a serving plate.

10 To make the icing, add enough lemon juice to the icing sugar to make a thick, spreadable icing. Pour over the cake and spread to the edges. Decorate with lemon shreds.

Energy 356kcal/1491kJ; Protein 6.7g; Carbohydrate 43.6g, of which sugars 29.8g; Fat 18.4g, of which saturates 4g; Cholesterol 118mg; Calcium 68mg; Fibre 0.6g; Sodium 227mg.

Apple strudel

The apfelstrudel – wafer-thin pastry layers with a luscious chopped apple filling – was first baked by the Hungarians, and then adopted by the Viennese. The longer sheets of filo are best for this recipe, but if you cannot find these, use two small sheets and overlap them. Eat fresh.

SERVES 8–10

900g/2lb cooking apples
finely grated rind and juice
   of 1 lemon
50g/2oz/½ cup caster
   (superfine) sugar
75g/3oz/½ cup sultanas
   (golden raisins)
115g/4oz/½ cup unsalted butter,
   plus extra for greasing
75g/3oz white bread made
   into crumbs
50g/2oz/¼ cup flaked
   (sliced) almonds
2.5ml/½ tsp mixed (apple pie)
   spice
400g/14oz filo pastry, thawed
   if frozen
icing (confectioners') sugar,
   for dusting

1 Peel, core and slice the apples. Put them in a pan with the lemon rind and juice and the sugar. Cook over a medium heat for 8–10 minutes, or until tender. Put in a bowl, add the sultanas and cool for 30 minutes.

2 Preheat the oven to 190°C/375°F/ Gas 5. Grease a large baking sheet.

FILO PASTRY TIPS
• If using two sheets of filo in place of one, overlap them along the short end by about 2cm/¾in after you have brushed them with butter.
• Keep any unused sheets of filo covered with a damp cloth to prevent them from drying out.

3 Melt 30ml/2 tbsp of the butter in a pan, add the breadcrumbs and cook, stirring, until golden brown. Stir in the almonds and spice. Cook for 1 minute, then set aside to cool.

4 Melt the remaining butter and brush over a large filo sheet. Reserve two sheets for decoration. Continue to butter the sheets and layer them on top of the first sheet. Brush the top layer with butter.

5 Sprinkle half the crumb mixture over, leaving a 5cm/2in border at the edges. Top with the cooked apples, then with the remaining crumbs.

6 Fold in the sides, then roll up like a Swiss roll (jelly roll) to enclose the filling. Put on the prepared baking sheet, join side down.

7 Make ruffles from the reserved filo and arrange on top. Brush all over with butter and bake for 25–30 minutes, or until light golden and crisp.

8 Cool slightly, dust with icing sugar and serve warm or cold with crème fraîche or plain (natural) yogurt.

Energy 397kcal/1676kJ; Protein 5.3g; Carbohydrate 66g, of which sugars 30.7g; Fat 14.4g, of which saturates 8.7g; Cholesterol 35mg; Calcium 82mg; Fibre 3.1g; Sodium 196mg.

Streusel-topped peach cake

When it's not the season for fresh summer fruits you can still have a hint of the warmer days of the year by making this continental cake that uses canned peaches from the store cupboard. It also works well with canned apricots or black cherries. Serve fresh with thick cream.

SERVES 8–10

75g/3oz/6 tbsp butter, softened, plus extra for greasing
225g/8oz/2 cups self-raising (self-rising) flour
5ml/1 tsp baking powder
2.5ml/½ tsp ground cinnamon
75g/3oz/6 tbsp golden caster (superfine) sugar
finely grated rind of 1 orange
1 egg, beaten
150ml/¼ pt/⅔ cup milk

For the topping
75g/3oz/⅔ cup self-raising (self-rising) flour
50g/2oz/½ cup unsalted butter, diced
25g/1oz/2 tbsp demerara (raw) sugar

For the filling
400g/14oz can peach slices in juice, drained

1 Preheat the oven to 190°C/375°F/ Gas 5. Grease the base and sides of a 20cm/8in loose-based cake tin (pan) and line with baking parchment.

2 To make the topping, put the flour in a bowl or food processor, add the butter and process or rub in until fine crumbs form, then stir in the demerara sugar.

COOK'S TIP
This cake will keep for 2 days. It is not suitable for freezing.

3 To make the cake, sift the flour, baking powder and cinnamon into a large bowl.

4 Add all the remaining cake ingredients and beat together until smooth. Spoon into the tin and smooth the top level.

5 Cover the top with an even layer of drained peach slices.

6 Sprinkle the crumb topping over the peaches.

7 Bake for 40 minutes, or until golden and a skewer inserted into the centre comes out clean.

8 Cool in the tin for 5 minutes, then carefully remove the sides of the tin and cool the cake on a wire rack. Remove the lining paper.

Energy 244kcal/1034kJ; Protein 4.7g; Carbohydrate 46.7g, of which sugars 39.4g; Fat 5g, of which saturates 0.8g; Cholesterol 71mg; Calcium 47mg; Fibre 0.9g; Sodium 32mg.

Pear and cardamom spice cake

Fresh pears and cardamom, a classic combination of flavours, are used together in this moist fruit and nut cake that has added crunch from the poppy seeds. It makes a delicious and mouthwatering dessert when served with cream. This cake keeps in an airtight container for up to five days.

SERVES 8–12

115g/4oz/½ cup butter, plus extra
 for greasing
115g/4oz/generous ½ cup caster
 (superfine) sugar
2 eggs, beaten
225g/8oz/2 cups plain
 (all-purpose) flour
15ml/1 tbsp baking powder
30ml/2 tbsp milk
crushed seeds from 2 cardamom
 pods (beans)
50g/2oz/½ cup walnuts, chopped
15ml/1 tbsp poppy seeds
500g/1¼lb dessert pears, peeled,
 cored and thinly sliced
3 walnut halves
45ml/3 tbsp clear honey

1 Preheat the oven to 180°C/350°F/ Gas 4. Grease and line a 20cm/ 8in round deep cake tin (pan) with baking parchment.

2 In a bowl, beat the butter and sugar together until pale and light. Beat in the eggs a little at a time.

3 Sift the flour and baking powder together over the butter and sugar mixture, then fold in with the milk.

4 Stir in the cardamom seeds, chopped nuts and poppy seeds. Reserve one-third of the pear slices, and chop the remainder. Fold the chopped pears into the creamed mixture.

5 Transfer the batter to the prepared tin and smooth the top, making a small dip in the centre.

6 Put the walnut halves in the centre and fan the reserved pear slices around them, overlapping each slice and covering the batter.

7 Bake for 1¼–1½ hours, or until a skewer inserted in the centre comes out clean.

8 Leave the cake to cool in the tin for 20 minutes, turn out and then transfer to a wire rack. Remove the lining paper.

9 While the cake is warm, use a soft pastry brush and glaze the cake top with a generous quantity of clear honey. Leave to go cold.

Energy 231kcal/970kJ; Protein 3.7g; Carbohydrate 29g, of which sugars 14.7g; Fat 12g, of which saturates 5.5g; Cholesterol 52.3mg; Calcium 49mg; Fibre 1.6g; Sodium 73.5mg.

Pineapple and ginger upside-down cake

This light and moist cake has a sticky ginger glaze over stem ginger and pineapple pieces, which are arranged in the cake tin before the cake batter is added. It is superb served warm as a dessert with home-made custard or thick cream. This cake will keep refrigerated, for two days.

SERVES 8

20g/¾oz/1½ tbsp butter, plus extra
  for greasing
2 pieces preserved stem ginger,
  chopped, plus 60ml/4 tbsp syrup
450g/1lb can pineapple pieces in
  natural juice, drained
250g/9oz/2¼ cups wholemeal
  (whole-wheat) self-raising
  (self-rising) flour
15ml/1 tbsp baking powder
5ml/1 tsp ground ginger
5ml/1 tsp ground cinnamon
115g/4oz/½ cup soft light
  brown sugar
250ml/8fl oz/1 cup milk
45ml/3 tbsp sunflower oil
1 banana, peeled

1 Preheat the oven to 180°C/235°F/ Gas 4. Grease and line a 20cm/8in round deep cake tin (pan).

2 Melt the butter in a small pan over a gentle heat, then stir in the ginger syrup. Turn up the heat until the liquid thickens.

3 Pour the mixture into the prepared tin and smooth out to the sides.

4 Arrange the stem ginger, and one-third of the pineapple pieces, in the syrup in the tin. Set aside.

5 Sift together the flour, baking powder and spices into a large bowl, then stir in the sugar.

6 In a food processor or blender, blend together the milk, oil, the remaining pineapple and the banana until almost smooth, then add this mixture to the flour. Stir until thoroughly combined.

7 Spoon the mixture over the pineapple and ginger pieces in the tin and smooth level.

8 Bake for 45 minutes, or until a skewer inserted into the centre of the cake comes out clean. Leave to cool slightly, then place a serving plate over the tin and turn upside down. Remove the lining.

Energy 358kcal/1508kJ; Protein 4.6g; Carbohydrate 55.2g, of which sugars 47.1g; Fat 14.8g, of which saturates 8.3g; Cholesterol 126mg; Calcium 63mg; Fibre 1g; Sodium 126mg.

Pecan cake

Ground pecan nuts give this light cake a mellow flavour, which is further enriched with butter and honey drizzled over the cake once cooked. Serve with a dollop of whipped cream to make an unusual dessert. Keep refrigerated for up to three days.

6 Fold the beaten whites into the butter mixture, then gently fold in the flour and nut mixture.

7 Spoon the batter into the prepared tin and bake for 30 minutes, or until a skewer inserted in the centre comes out clean.

8 Allow the cake to cool in the tin for 5 minutes, then turn out on to a wire rack to go cold. Remove the lining paper. Arrange the pecan nuts on top of the cake. Transfer to a serving plate.

SERVES 8

115g/4oz/½ cup butter, softened, plus extra for greasing
115g/4oz/1 cup pecan nuts
75g/3oz/¾ cup plain (all-purpose) flour
115g/4oz/½ cup soft light brown sugar
5ml/1 tsp vanilla extract
4 large (US extra large) eggs, separated
pinch of salt
12 whole pecan nuts, to decorate
whipped cream, to serve

For drizzling
50g/2oz/¼ cup butter
120ml/4fl oz/scant ½ cup clear (runny) honey

1 Preheat the oven to 180°C/350°F/ Gas 4. Grease and line a 20cm/8in round shallow cake tin (pan) with baking parchment.

2 Toast the pecan nuts in a dry frying pan for 5 minutes, shaking frequently.

3 Grind the nuts finely in a blender or food processor. Stir in the flour.

4 In a mixing bowl, beat the butter and sugar together until light and fluffy, then beat in the vanilla extract and egg yolks.

5 Put the egg whites and salt into a clean, grease-free bowl and whisk until they form soft peaks.

9 Melt the butter for drizzling in a small pan, add the honey and bring to the boil, stirring. Lower the heat and simmer for 3 minutes. Pour over the cake. Serve with whipped cream.

Energy 428kcal/1785kJ; Protein 6.2g; Carbohydrate 34.7g, of which sugars 27.4g; Fat 30.5g, of which saturates 12.5g; Cholesterol 158mg; Calcium 51mg; Fibre 1g; Sodium 170mg.

Almond cake

Toasted almonds are the main ingredient in this light cake, giving it a nutty flavour and an excellent texture. It is best served warm, and a scoop of vanilla or good-quality chocolate ice cream would also go well with it. Eat this fresh, or keep it for one day in an airtight container.

SERVES 4–6

25g/1oz/2 tbsp butter, plus extra
   for greasing
225/8oz/2 cups blanched
   whole almonds
75g/3oz/¾ cup icing (confectioners')
   sugar, plus extra for dusting
3 eggs
2.5ml/½ tsp almond extract
25g/1oz/¼ cup plain
   (all-purpose) flour
3 egg whites
15ml/1 tbsp caster (superfine)
   sugar

4 Add the whole eggs and the remaining icing sugar to the bowl. With an electric whisk, beat until the mixture forms a trail when the beaters are lifted away.

5 In a small pan, melt the butter, then mix into the nut and egg mixture with the almond extract.

6 Sift over the flour and fold in.

7 Whisk the egg whites into a clean, grease-free bowl until they form soft peaks. Add the sugar. Beat until stiff.

1 Preheat the oven to 160°C/325°F/Gas 3. Grease and line a 23cm/9in round shallow cake tin (pan) with baking parchment.

2 Spread the almonds in an even layer in a baking tray and bake for 10 minutes. Allow the almonds to cool. Set aside a few of the almonds for decoration. Chop the rest, then grind them with half of the icing sugar in a food processor. Transfer to a large bowl.

3 Increase the oven temperature to 200°C/400°F/Gas 6.

8 Fold the egg whites into the batter. Spoon into the cake tin. Bake for 15–20 minutes, until golden. Turn out of the tin. Remove the papers.

9 Decorate with the toasted almonds and dust with icing sugar.

Energy 376kcal/1568kJ; Protein 13g; Carbohydrate 21.5g, of which sugars 17.3g; Fat 27.2g, of which saturates 4.6g; Cholesterol 104mg; Calcium 120mg; Fibre 2.9g; Sodium 97mg.

Walnut cake

Brandy, orange and cinnamon warmed in a sugar syrup are poured over this baked walnut cake, and this technique makes it superbly moist and full of complementary flavours. This cake is lovely served immediately, but will keep for three days in the refrigerator.

SERVES 10–12

150g/5oz/10 tbsp unsalted butter, plus extra for greasing
115g/4oz/generous ½ cup caster (superfine) sugar
4 eggs, separated
60ml/4 tbsp brandy
2.5ml/½ tsp ground cinnamon
300g/11oz/2¾ cups walnuts
150g/5oz/1¼ cups self-raising (self-rising) flour
5ml/1 tsp baking powder
pinch of salt

For the syrup
250g/9oz/1¼ cups caster (superfine) sugar
30ml/2 tbsp brandy
2 or 3 strips of pared orange rind
2 cinnamon sticks

1 Preheat the oven to 190°C/375°F/ Gas 5. Grease and line a 35 × 23cm/ 14 × 9in shallow cake tin (pan).

2 In a bowl, beat the butter and sugar together until light and fluffy. Beat in the egg yolks one at a time. Stir in the brandy and cinnamon.

3 Coarsely chop the walnuts, using a food processor, and stir them in.

4 Sift the flour with the baking powder and set aside.

5 Put the egg whites and salt into a clean, grease-free bowl and whisk until they form stiff peaks.

6 Fold the egg whites into the butter and sugar mixture, alternating with tablespoons of flour.

7 Spread the batter evenly in the prepared tin. Bake for about 40 minutes, or until the top is golden and a skewer inserted into the centre comes out clean. Set on a wire rack in the tin.

8 To make the syrup, mix the sugar and 300ml/½ pint/1¼ cups water in a small pan. Heat gently, stirring, until the sugar has dissolved. Bring to the boil, lower the heat and add the brandy, orange rind and cinnamon sticks. Simmer for 10 minutes.

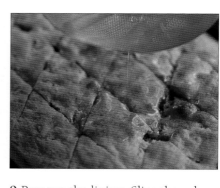

9 Remove the lining. Slice the cake into diamonds while still hot and strain the syrup over it. Let it stand for 10–20 minutes, then turn out on to a wire rack to go cold.

Energy 563kcal/2349kJ; Protein 8.5g; Carbohydrate 50.6g, of which sugars 39.2g; Fat 35.3g, of which saturates 10.1g; Cholesterol 108mg; Calcium 114mg; Fibre 1.5g; Sodium 177mg.

Pine nut and almond cake

This unusual recipe uses olive oil, toasted semolina and nuts to give the cake a rich flavour and a dense, grainy texture. It is also incredibly moist because it is soaked in a cinnamon and sugar syrup. Unlike traditional cakes it is not baked in the oven, but heated in a pan. Eat fresh.

SERVES 6–8

500g/1¼lb/2¾ cups caster
   (superfine) sugar
1 cinnamon stick
250ml/8fl oz/1 cup olive oil
350g/12oz/2 cups coarse semolina
50g/2oz/½ cup blanched almonds
30ml/2 tbsp pine nuts
5ml/1 tsp ground cinnamon

1 Put the sugar in a heavy pan with 1 litre/1¾ pints/4 cups cold water and the cinnamon stick. Bring to the boil, stirring until the sugar dissolves, then boil without stirring for 4 minutes to make a syrup.

2 Meanwhile, heat the oil in a separate, heavy pan. When it is almost smoking, add the semolina gradually and stir constantly until it turns light brown.

3 Lower the heat, add the almonds and pine nuts, and brown together for 2–3 minutes, stirring constantly.

4 Take the semolina mixture off the heat and set aside. Remove the cinnamon stick from the hot syrup using a slotted spoon and discard it.

5 Carefully add the hot syrup to the semolina mixture, stirring all the time. The mixture will hiss and spit at this point, so stand well away from it.

6 Return the pan to a gentle heat and stir until the syrup has been absorbed and the mixture is smooth.

7 Remove the pan from the heat, cover it with a clean dish towel and leave it to stand for 10 minutes so that any remaining moisture is absorbed.

8 Spoon the mixture into a 20–23cm/ 8–9in round non-stick cake tin (pan), and set it aside. When cold, unmould it on to a platter and dust it all over with the cinnamon.

Energy 643kcal/2706kJ; Protein 6.8g; Carbohydrate 99.8g, of which sugars 65.7g; Fat 26.8g, of which saturates 3.3g; Cholesterol 0mg; Calcium 56mg; Fibre 1.5g; Sodium 10mg.

Poppy seed cake

This plain and simple cake is flavoured with lemon and vanilla and is packed with black poppy seeds – a popular ingredient for speciality breads. As well as giving the cake a good crunch, poppy seeds add a nutty and distinctive taste. Serve it with cream, and keep for up to three days.

3 Sift and fold the flour and baking powder into the egg and poppy seed mixture, in three batches, alternating with the milk.

4 Add the cooled, melted butter and the sunflower oil, and stir in.

SERVES 8

130g/4½oz/generous ½ cup
  unsalted butter, melted, plus
  extra for greasing
2 eggs
225g/8oz/generous 1 cup caster
  (superfine) sugar
5–10ml/1–2 tsp vanilla extract
200g/7oz/scant 1½ cups poppy
  seeds, ground
15ml/1 tbsp grated lemon rind
130g/4½oz/generous 1 cup
  self-raising (self-rising) flour
5ml/1 tsp baking powder
120ml/4fl oz/½ cup milk
30ml/2 tbsp sunflower oil
icing (confectioners') sugar, sifted,
  for dusting
whipped cream, to serve

1 Preheat the oven to 180°C/350°F/
Gas 4. Grease a 23cm/9in round
deep cake tin (pan).

2 In a large bowl, beat together the eggs, sugar and vanilla extract, using an electric whisk, for 4–5 minutes, or by hand until pale and fluffy. Stir in the poppy seeds and the lemon rind.

5 Pour the mixture into the tin and bake for 40 minutes, or until firm. Cool in the tin for 15 minutes, then invert on to a wire rack. Leave until cold, dust with icing sugar and serve with cream.

COOK'S TIP
Culinary poppy seeds have a distinctive nutty taste. To enhance the aroma and flavour, lightly toast them first.

Energy 485kcal/2023kJ; Protein 8.3g; Carbohydrate 42.7g, of which sugars 30.5g; Fat 32.4g, of which saturates 11.4g; Cholesterol 83mg; Calcium 267mg; Fibre 2.5g; Sodium 188mg.

Date and walnut spice cake

This deliciously moist and rich spiced cake is topped with a sticky honey and orange glaze. Serve it as a dessert with a generous spoonful of natural yogurt, or crème fraîche, flavoured with grated orange rind. Keep this cake, refrigerated, for up to three days.

SERVES 8

115g/4oz/½ cup unsalted butter, plus extra for greasing
175g/6oz/¾ cup soft dark brown sugar
2 eggs
175g/6oz/1½ cups self-raising (self-rising) flour, plus extra for dusting
5ml/1 tsp bicarbonate of soda (baking soda)
2.5ml/½ tsp freshly grated nutmeg
5ml/1 tsp mixed spice
pinch of salt
175ml/6fl oz/¾ cup buttermilk
50g/2oz/⅓ cup ready-to-eat stoned (pitted) dates, chopped
25g/1oz/¼ cup walnuts, chopped

For the topping
60ml/4 tbsp clear honey
45ml/3 tbsp fresh orange juice
15ml/1 tbsp coarsely grated orange rind

1 Preheat the oven to 180°C/350°F/Gas 4. Grease and lightly flour a 23cm/9in round deep cake tin (pan).

2 In a bowl, beat the butter and sugar until light and fluffy, then beat in the eggs one at a time.

3 Sift together the flour, bicarbonate of soda, spices and salt into a bowl.

4 Add the flour mixture to the egg and sugar mixture, alternating with the buttermilk, and stir well to combine. Add the dates and walnuts, and mix in.

5 Spoon the batter into the prepared cake tin and smooth the top level.

6 Bake for 50 minutes, or until a skewer inserted into the centre comes out clean. Leave to cool for 5 minutes. Turn out on to a wire rack to go cold.

7 To make the topping, heat the honey, orange juice and rind in a pan. Bring to the boil. Boil rapidly, without stirring, for 3 minutes, or until syrupy.

8 Prick holes in the top of the cake and pour over the hot syrup.

Energy 350kcal/1472kJ; Protein 5.1g; Carbohydrate 50.3g, of which sugars 34.1g; Fat 15.7g, of which saturates 8.1g; Cholesterol 79mg; Calcium 131mg; Fibre 1g; Sodium 196mg.

Gâteaux, Meringues and Pastries

Many of us have been tempted to buy beautiful gâteaux, meringues or pastries from a pâtisserie and serve these as a dessert for a special occasion, but you can also create these elegant specialities in your own kitchen. These do take a little more time and effort to make than many other cakes, but most can be prepared ahead or in stages. Although the cakes look a little more complicated, you will be surprised how simple skills can achieve a spectacular, mouthwatering centrepiece.

Lemon roulade with lemon-curd cream

This feather-light roulade is flavoured with almonds and filled with a rich lemon-curd cream. It makes a marvellous summer dessert. Use best-quality or home-made lemon curd for that perfect touch. Eat this cake fresh for the best taste. It will store chilled for 1–2 days.

SERVES 8

butter, for greasing
4 eggs, separated
115g/4oz/generous ½ cup caster
   (superfine) sugar
finely grated rind of 2 lemons,
   plus extra to decorate
5ml/1 tsp vanilla extract
40g/1½oz/⅓ cup plain
   (all-purpose) flour
25g/1oz/¼ cup ground almonds

For the lemon-curd cream
300ml/½ pint/1¼ cups double
   (heavy) cream
60ml/4 tbsp lemon curd
45ml/3 tbsp icing (confectioners')
   sugar, for dusting

1 Preheat the oven to 190°C/375°F/ Gas 5. Grease and line a 33 × 23cm/ 13 × 9in Swiss roll tin (jelly roll pan) with baking parchment.

2 In a large bowl, beat the egg yolks with half the sugar until foamy. Beat in the lemon rind and vanilla extract.

3 Sift the flour over the egg mixture and lightly fold in with the ground almonds, using a metal spoon.

4 Put the egg whites into a clean, grease-free bowl and whisk until they form stiff, glossy peaks.

5 Gradually whisk in the remaining sugar to form a stiff meringue.

6 Stir half the meringue mixture into the egg yolk mixture to slacken it. When combined, fold in the remainder of the meringue mixture.

7 Pour the batter into the prepared tin and smooth level.

8 Bake for 10 minutes, or until risen and spongy to the touch.

9 Put the tin on a wire rack and cover loosely with a sheet of baking parchment and a damp dish towel. Leave to cool.

10 To make the lemon curd-cream, whip the cream until it holds its shape, then fold in the lemon cream.

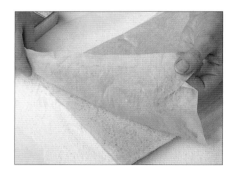

11 Sift the icing sugar over a piece of baking parchment. Turn the sponge out on to it. Peel off the lining paper and spread over the filling.

12 Using the paper, roll up the sponge from one long side. Sprinkle with lemon rind.

Energy 337kcal/1401kJ; Protein 5g; Carbohydrate 24.5g, of which sugars 18.9g; Fat 25.1g, of which saturates 13.6g; Cholesterol 148mg; Calcium 55mg; Fibre 0.4g; Sodium 50mg.

Layer cake

Three light cakes enclose one layer of crushed raspberries and another of custard, then the whole cake is covered with vanilla-flavoured cream. Make when raspberries are at their sweetest and best. Bake the cake layers the day before for the best flavour, then assemble the cake and eat it fresh.

SERVES 10–12

115g/4oz/½ cup unsalted butter, plus extra for greasing
200g/7oz/1 cup caster (superfine) sugar
4 eggs, separated
45ml/3 tbsp milk
175g/6oz/1½ cups plain (all-purpose) flour
25ml/1½ tbsp cornflour (cornstarch)
7.5ml/1½ tsp baking powder
5ml/1 tsp vanilla sugar
fresh raspberries, to decorate

For the custard filling
2 eggs
90g/3½oz/½ cup caster (superfine) sugar
15ml/1 tbsp cornflour (cornstarch)
350ml/12fl oz/1½ cups milk

For the cream topping
475ml/16fl oz/2 cups double (heavy) cream or whipping cream
25g/1oz/½ cup icing (confectioners') sugar
5ml/1 tsp vanilla sugar

For the raspberry filling
375g/13oz/generous 2 cups raspberries
sugar, to taste

COOK'S TIP
To make vanilla sugar, put a vanilla pod in a jar with a well-fitting lid, and fill with caster (superfine) sugar.

1 Preheat the oven to 230°C/450°F/Gas 8. Lightly grease and flour three 23cm/9in shallow cake tins (pans).

2 Cream the butter with the sugar in a large bowl until light and fluffy. Beat in the egg yolks, one at a time. Stir in the milk until blended.

3 In a separate bowl, sift together the flour, cornflour, baking powder and vanilla sugar. Beat the flour mixture into the egg mixture.

4 Put the egg whites into a clean, grease-free bowl and whisk until they form stiff peaks. Gently fold the egg whites into the cake mixture.

5 Divide the batter evenly among the tins and smooth to the edges. Bake for 12 minutes. Leave the cakes to cool for 10 minutes, then turn out to go cold on a wire rack.

6 To make the custard filling, whisk together the eggs and sugar in a pan. Whisk in the cornflour and the milk. Cook over a low heat, stirring, for about 6 minutes or until thickened. Remove from the heat and leave to cool.

7 Beat the cream in a bowl until soft peaks form. Stir in the icing sugar and vanilla sugar and continue beating until stiff.

8 To make the raspberry filling, crush the raspberries in a bowl and add a little sugar to taste.

9 To assemble the cake, place one layer on a serving plate and spread with the raspberry filling.

10 Place a second cake layer over the first and spread with the cooled custard. Top with the final layer.

11 Spread whipped cream over the sides and top of the cake.

12 Chill the cake until ready to serve, and decorate with raspberries.

Energy 433kcal/1811kJ; Protein 6.1g; Carbohydrate 44.6g, of which sugars 30.4g; Fat 27g, of which saturates 15.9g; Cholesterol 157mg; Calcium 86mg; Fibre 1.2g; Sodium 109mg.

Sponge cake with strawberries and cream

This classic treat is delicious in the summer, filled with ripe, fragrant strawberries. The sponge is exceptionally light because it is made without fat. To ensure you have a perfect sponge, have all the ingredients at room temperature. Eat this cake on the day it is made.

SERVES 8–10

oil, for greasing
115g/4oz/generous ½ cup caster (superfine) sugar, plus extra for dusting
90g/3½oz/¾ cup plain (all-purpose) flour, sifted, plus extra for dusting
4 eggs
icing (confectioners') sugar, for dusting

For the filling
300ml/½ pint/1¼ cups double (heavy) cream
about 5ml/1 tsp icing (confectioners') sugar, sifted
450g/1lb/4 cups strawberries, washed and hulled
a little orange liqueur (optional)

1 Preheat the oven to 190°C/375°F/ Gas 5. Grease a round 20cm/8in cake tin (pan). Dust the tin with 10ml/2 tsp caster sugar and flour combined. Tap out the excess.

COOK'S TIP
Freeze, unfilled, for 2 months.

2 Put the eggs and sugar into a bowl and use an electric whisk at high speed until the mixture is light and thick, and the mixture leaves a trail as it drops from the whisk. (To whisk by hand: set the bowl over a pan one quarter filled with hot water and whisk until thick and creamy, then remove from the heat.)

3 Sift the flour over the whisked eggs and carefully fold it in with a metal spoon, mixing thoroughly but losing as little volume as possible.

4 Pour the batter into the cake tin and smooth the top level. Bake for 25–30 minutes, or until the sponge feels springy to the touch.

5 Leave in the tin for 5 minutes to set slightly, then loosen the sides with a knife and invert on to a wire rack to go cold.

6 To make the filling, whip the cream with a little icing sugar until it is stiff enough to hold its shape.

7 Slice the sponge across the middle with a long sharp knife to make two even layers.

8 Divide half the cream between the two inner cut sides of the sandwich.

9 Reserve some strawberries for the cake top, and then slice the rest.

10 Put the first sponge half on a serving plate and arrange the sliced strawberries on the cream. Sprinkle with liqueur, if using.

11 Cover with the second cake half and press down gently.

12 Spread the remaining cream on top of the cake, and arrange the reserved strawberries, whole or halved according to size, on top.

13 Set aside for an hour or so for the flavours to develop, then dust lightly with icing sugar and serve.

Energy 333kcal/1387kJ; Protein 5.3g; Carbohydrate 27.8g, of which sugars 19.2g; Fat 23.1g, of which saturates 13.3g; Cholesterol 147mg; Calcium 65mg; Fibre 1g; Sodium 48mg.

Cinnamon apple gâteau

Make this unusual cake for an autumn dessert. A light sponge is split and filled with a honey and cream cheese layer as well as softly cooked cinnamon apples and sultanas, then topped with glazed apples. Keep the sponge, unfilled, for two days in an airtight container; fill and eat it fresh.

SERVES 8–10

butter, for greasing
3 eggs
115g/4oz/generous ½ cup caster
   (superfine) sugar
75g/3oz/⅔ cup plain
   (all-purpose) flour
5ml/1 tsp ground cinnamon

For the filling and topping
4 large eating apples
60ml/4 tbsp clear honey
75g/3oz/generous ½ cup sultanas
   (golden raisins)
2.5ml/½ tsp ground cinnamon
350g/12oz/1½ cups soft cheese
60ml/4 tbsp fromage frais or
   crème fraîche
10ml/2 tsp lemon juice
45ml/3 tbsp apricot jam, strained
mint sprigs, to decorate

1 Preheat the oven to 190°C/ 375°F/Gas 5. Grease and line a 23cm/9in round cake tin (pan) with baking parchment.

2 Put the eggs and sugar in a bowl and beat with an electric whisk until thick and mousse-like and the beaters leave a trail on the surface.

3 Sift the flour and cinnamon over the egg mixture and carefully fold in with a large spoon.

4 Pour into the prepared tin and bake for 25–30 minutes, or until the cake springs back when lightly pressed in the centre.

5 Slide a knife between the cake and the tin to loosen the edge, then turn the cake on to a wire rack to cool.

6 To make the filling, peel, core and slice three apples and put them in a pan. Add 30ml/ 2 tbsp of the honey and 15ml/1 tbsp water. Cover and cook over a low heat for 10 minutes, or until the apples have softened.

7 Add the sultanas and cinnamon, stir, replace the lid and leave to cool.

8 Put the soft cheese in a bowl with the remaining honey, the fromage frais or crème fraîche and half the lemon juice. Beat until smooth.

9 Cut the cake into two equal rounds. Put half on a plate and drizzle over any liquid from the apple mixture.

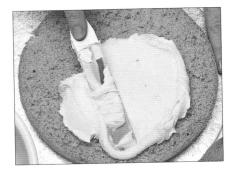

10 Spread with two-thirds of the cheese mixture, then top with the apple filling. Fit the top of the cake in place.

11 Swirl the remaining cheese mixture over the top of the sponge. Core and slice the remaining apple, sprinkle with lemon juice and use to decorate the edge of the cake. Brush the apple with apricot glaze and place mint sprigs on top to decorate.

Energy 239kcal/1010kJ; Protein 10.8g; Carbohydrate 39.9g, of which sugars 32.8g; Fat 5.8g, of which saturates 2.9g; Cholesterol 82mg; Calcium 97mg; Fibre 1.1g; Sodium 225mg.

Raspberry and hazelnut meringue cake

Toasted and ground hazelnuts add a nutty flavour to this simple cake of meringue rounds sandwiched together with fresh cream and raspberries. This combination will appeal to all dessert lovers. Store the baked meringue bases, unfilled, for one week. Once filled, eat fresh.

SERVES 8

butter, for greasing
140g/5oz/1¼ cups hazelnuts
4 egg whites
200g/7oz/1 cup caster
   (superfine) sugar
2.5ml/½ tsp vanilla extract

For the filling
300ml/½ pint/1¼ cups
   whipping cream
700g/1lb 8oz/4 cups raspberries

1 Preheat the oven to 180°C/350°F/ Gas 4. Grease and line the bases of two 20cm/8in round cake tins (pans) with baking parchment.

2 Spread the hazelnuts on a baking sheet and bake for 8 minutes, or until lightly toasted. Leave to cool slightly. Rub the hazelnuts vigorously in a clean dish towel to remove the skins. Reduce the oven temperature to 150°C/ 300°F/Gas 2.

3 Grind the nuts in a food processor, until they are the consistency of coarse sand.

4 Put the egg whites into a clean, grease-free bowl and whisk until they form stiff peaks. Beat in 30ml/ 2 tbsp of the sugar, then, using a plastic spatula, fold in the remaining sugar, a few spoonfuls at a time.

5 Fold in the vanilla and hazelnuts.

6 Divide the mixture between the cake tins and smooth the top level. Bake for 1¼ hours until firm.

7 Leave to cool in the tin for 5 minutes, then run a knife around the inside edge of the tins to loosen the meringues. Turn out to go cold on a wire rack.

8 For the filling, whip the cream. Spread half on one cake round and top with half the raspberries.

9 Top with the other cake round. Spread the remaining cream on top and arrange the rest of the raspberries over the surface. Chill for 1 hour before serving.

Energy 298kcal/1252kJ; Protein 3.2g; Carbohydrate 39.5g, of which sugars 39.5g; Fat 15.3g, of which saturates 9.5g; Cholesterol 39mg; Calcium 55mg; Fibre 1.4g; Sodium 44mg.

Griestorte with pineapple filling

This classic continental gâteau uses semolina and ground almonds for a deliciously short, crunchy texture. The filling of cream, pineapple and chocolate makes a soft, tangy contrast to the cake. Bake the base a day ahead, or bake and freeze it unfilled. Eat fresh once filled.

SERVES 8

butter, for greasing
3 eggs, separated
115g/4oz/generous ½ cup caster
  (superfine) sugar
juice and finely grated rind
  of ½ lemon
30ml/2 tbsp ground almonds
50g/2oz/⅓ cup fine semolina
icing (confectioners') sugar,
  for dusting
chocolate curls or flakes, to
  decorate, *see page 64*

For the filling
300ml/½ pint/1½ cups double
  (heavy) cream
4 slices canned pineapple, drained
  and chopped
75g/3oz dark (bittersweet)
  chocolate, coarsely grated

1 Preheat the oven to 180°C/350°F/
Gas 4. Grease and line a 20cm/8in
round deep cake tin (pan) with
baking parchment.

2 Whisk the egg yolks with the
sugar and lemon rind until pale
and light. Add the lemon juice.
Whisk until thick and the mixture
leaves a ribbon trail when the
whisk is lifted.

3 Fold in the almonds and semolina.

4 Put the egg whites into a clean,
grease-free bowl and whisk until
they form soft peaks, then fold into
the yolk mixture in three batches.

5 Spoon into the prepared tin and
bake for 30–35 minutes, or until
risen and pale golden. Cool in the
tin for 5 minutes. Turn the cake out
on to a wire rack and cool
completely. Remove the papers. Cut
the cake in half horizontally.

6 Whip the cream until it holds its
shape, then fold in the pineapple and
chocolate. Use the cream to sandwich
the cakes together. Dust the top with
icing sugar, and decorate with
chocolate curls.

Energy 356kcal/1484kJ; Protein 5g; Carbohydrate 29.7g, of which sugars 24.2g; Fat 27.2g, of which saturates 13.6g; Cholesterol 121mg; Calcium 52mg; Fibre 0.5g; Sodium 44mg.

Summer celebration shortcake

A departure from the usual summer shortcake, this crisp dessert contains crunchy almonds, which go particularly well with the juicy strawberries and cream filling. The top layer is already divided into portions, giving it an attractive appearance as well as making it easier to serve.

SERVES 8

175g/6oz/¾ cup butter, plus extra
   for greasing
150g/5oz/1¼ cups plain
   (all-purpose) flour
115g/4oz/1 cup ground almonds
50g/2oz/¼ cup caster
   (superfine) sugar
25g/1oz/¼ cup flaked
   (sliced) almonds

For the filling and decoration
450g/1lb/4 cups fresh strawberries
300ml/½ pint/1¼ cups double
   (heavy) cream
15ml/1 tbsp amaretto (optional)
icing (confectioners') sugar,
   for dusting

1 Preheat the oven to 180°C/350°F/ Gas 4. Grease two baking sheets.

2 Rub the butter into the flour until it resembles fine breadcrumbs, then stir in the ground almonds and caster sugar. Mix to form a soft dough, then transfer to a floured surface, and knead until smooth.

3 Roll half of the dough into a 20cm/8in round and cut out neatly. Put on a baking sheet and sprinkle over half the almonds. Knead the trimmings and the rest of the dough to make a second shortcake round. Sprinkle over the almonds. Prick each with a fork.

4 Bake for 20 minutes, or until pale golden. Mark the flattest one into eight triangles while warm, and leave to cool. Cut the triangles when cold.

5 For the filling, reserve nine strawberries. Hull and chop the rest. Whip the cream until it forms soft peaks. Place one quarter in a piping (pastry) bag fitted with a star nozzle.

6 Fold the berries into the remaining cream with the liqueur, if using.

7 Put the whole shortbread on a serving plate. Pile the fruit filling on top and arrange the eight triangles on top with points facing inwards.

8 Pipe a cream rosette on each one and top with a strawberry. Put the last strawberry in the centre. Dust lightly with icing sugar. Serve immediately.

Energy 364kcal/1515kJ; Protein 4.3g; Carbohydrate 29.9g, of which sugars 8.5g; Fat 25.6g, of which saturates 15.6g; Cholesterol 87mg; Calcium 70mg; Fibre 1.2g; Sodium 76mg.

White chocolate cappuccino gâteau

A fabulous dessert for a special occasion, this gâteau is made with light sponge layers filled with coffee liqueur cream. On top is a fluffy coating of white chocolate and coffee liqueur frosting, with a layer of chocolate curls dusted with cocoa. This will keep chilled, for two days.

SERVES 8

butter, for greasing
4 eggs
115g/4oz/generous ½ cup caster (superfine) sugar
15ml/1 tbsp strong black coffee
2.5ml/½ tsp vanilla extract
115g/4oz/1 cup plain (all-purpose) flour
75g/3oz white chocolate, grated
white chocolate curls, to decorate, *see page 64*
unsweetened cocoa powder or powdered cinnamon, for dusting

For the filling
120ml/4fl oz/½ cup double (heavy) cream
15ml/1 tbsp coffee liqueur

For the white chocolate frosting
175g/6oz white chocolate
75g/3oz/6 tbsp unsalted butter
115g/4oz/1 cup icing (confectioners') sugar
90ml/6 tbsp double (heavy) cream
15ml/1 tbsp coffee liqueur

1 Preheat the oven to 180°C/350°F/ Gas 4. Grease and line two 18cm/ 7in round shallow cake tins (pans).

2 Combine the eggs, sugar, coffee and vanilla extract in a large bowl set over a pan of hot water. Whisk until the mixture is pale and holds its shape when the beaters are lifted.

3 Sift half the flour over the mixture, and fold in. Fold in the rest of the flour with the grated chocolate.

4 Divide between the cake tins. Bake for 20–25 minutes, until golden. Turn out to cool on wire racks.

5 Whip the filling ingredients in a bowl until stiff. Spread over one cake and put the second cake on top.

6 To make the frosting, melt the chocolate with the butter in a heatproof bowl set over a pan of simmering water. Remove from the heat and beat in the icing sugar.

7 Whip the cream in another bowl until it just holds its shape, then beat into the chocolate mixture. Allow to cool, stirring occasionally. Stir in the coffee liqueur.

8 Spread over the top and sides of the cake. Top with white chocolate curls and dust with cocoa or cinnamon. Freeze any leftover slices wrapped in foil.

Energy 337kcal/1418kJ; Protein 5.3g; Carbohydrate 50.5g, of which sugars 39.5g; Fat 13.6g, of which saturates 7.4g; Cholesterol 116mg; Calcium 61mg; Fibre 0.7g; Sodium 41mg.

Coconut lime gâteau

American frosting is what makes this zesty lime and coconut gâteau so attractive. Made by whisking egg white and a sugar mixture over heat, the frosting is like a soft meringue icing. It tastes divine scattered with toasted coconut. Eat the gâteau fresh or refrigerate it for two days.

SERVES 10–12

225g/8oz/1 cup butter, at
  room temperature, plus extra
  for greasing
225g/8oz/2 cups plain
  (all-purpose) flour
12.5ml/2½ tsp baking powder
225g/8oz/generous 1 cup caster
  (superfine) sugar
grated rind of 2 limes
4 eggs
60ml/4 tbsp fresh lime juice (from
  about 2 limes)
85g/3oz/1 cup desiccated (dry
  unsweetened shredded) coconut

For the frosting
275g/10oz/scant 1½ cups caster
  (superfine) sugar
2.5ml/½ tsp cream of tartar
2 egg whites
60ml/4 tbsp cold water
15ml/1 tbsp liquid glucose
10ml/2 tsp vanilla extract

1 Preheat the oven to 180°C/350°F/ Gas 4. Grease and line two 23cm/9in round shallow cake tins (pans) with baking parchment.

2 Sift together the flour and baking powder into a bowl.

3 In another large bowl, beat the butter until soft. Add the sugar and lime rind, then beat until pale and fluffy. Beat in the eggs, one at a time, adding 5ml/1 tsp of the flour mixture with each addition to stop the batter from curdling. Beat the mixture well between each addition.

4 Using a wooden spoon, fold in the flour mixture in small batches, alternating with the lime juice. When the batter is smooth, stir in two-thirds of the coconut.

5 Divide the batter between the tins and spread it evenly to the sides.

6 Bake for 30–35 minutes, or until a skewer inserted into the centre comes out clean. Leave to cool in the tins for 10 minutes, then turn out to cool on a wire rack. Remove the lining paper. Leave to go cold.

7 Spread the remaining coconut in another cake tin. Bake until golden brown, stirring occasionally. Watch carefully so that the coconut does not get too dark. Allow to cool in the tin.

8 To make the frosting, put the sugar in a large heatproof bowl and add the cream of tartar, egg whites, water and glucose. Stir to mix.

9 Set the bowl over a pan of boiling water. Beat with an electric whisk at high speed for 7 minutes or until thick and stiff peaks form. Remove from the heat.

10 Add the vanilla extract and continue beating for 3 minutes or until the frosting has cooled slightly.

11 Invert one cake on a serving plate. Spread a layer of frosting on top.

12 Set the second cake on top. Swirl the rest of the frosting all over the cake. Sprinkle with the toasted coconut and leave to set.

Energy 732kcal/3079kJ; Protein 7.3g; Carbohydrate 111g, of which sugars 59g; Fat 32g, of which saturates 20.5g; Cholesterol 155mg; Calcium 105.7mg; Fibre 2.1g; Sodium 221mg.

Angel food cake

Similar to a whisked sponge cake, the texture of this American classic is springy but slightly sticky, and the colour is snowy white. The cream of tartar helps to aerate the egg whites, and the addition of sugar creates a light meringue mixture. This will keep refrigerated, for up to five days.

SERVES 20

65g/2½oz/9 tbsp plain
  (all-purpose) flour
15ml/1 tbsp cornflour (cornstarch)
225g/8oz/generous 1 cup caster
  (superfine) sugar
10 egg whites
5ml/1 tsp cream of tartar
7.5ml/1½ tsp vanilla extract

For the frosting
2 egg whites
115g/4oz/generous ½ cup caster
  (superfine) sugar
10ml/2 tsp golden (light corn)
  syrup
2.5ml/½ tsp vanilla extract
rind of 1 orange, to decorate

1 Preheat the oven to 180°C/350°F/ Gas 4.

2 In a large bowl, sift together the flour, cornflour and 50g/2oz/¼ cup of the sugar three times, so that the texture is very, very light.

3 Put the egg whites and the cream of tartar into a clean, grease-free bowl and whisk until they form stiff peaks.

4 Gradually whisk in the remaining sugar, 15ml/1 tbsp at a time, until the mixture becomes thick and glossy.

5 Using a metal spoon, gently fold the sifted flour and the vanilla extract into the whisked egg whites until combined. Transfer the mixture to a 25cm/10in non-stick ring mould and smooth out the batter so that it is level.

6 Bake for 35–40 minutes, or until risen and golden. Remove from the oven, invert the cake in its mould on to a wire rack. Leave to go cold.

7 To make the frosting, put the egg whites into a clean, grease-free bowl. Whisk until stiff and dry, then set aside.

8 Heat the sugar and 60ml/4 tbsp water in a small pan, stirring constantly until the sugar dissolves.

9 Increase the heat and boil until the temperature reaches 115°C/240°F on a sugar thermometer. As soon as this temperature is reached, remove the pan from the heat.

10 Pour the syrup into the egg whites, whisking constantly, until the mixture is thick and glossy.

11 Beat in the golden syrup and vanilla, beating for 5 minutes.

12 Lift the mould off the cake and put the cake on a serving plate.

13 Quickly spread the frosting over the cake. Sprinkle with orange rind.

Energy 117kcal/500kJ; Protein 3.1g; Carbohydrate 27.7g, of which sugars 21.4g; Fat 0.1g, of which saturates 0g; Cholesterol 0mg; Calcium 24mg; Fibre 0.3g; Sodium 49mg.

Boston cream pie

Created by chef M. Sanzian at the Parker House Hotel in Boston, in the 1850s, this famous 'pie' is actually a cake. It is unusual, because sandwiched between the two cake layers is a rich custard. With its chocolate glaze it is really very appealing. Keep, refrigerated, for up to three days.

SERVES 8

butter, for greasing
225g/8oz/2 cups plain
   (all-purpose) four
15ml/1 tbsp baking powder
pinch of salt
115g/4oz/½ cup butter, softened,
   plus extra for greasing
200g/7oz/1 cup caster
   (superfine) sugar
2 eggs
5ml/1 tsp vanilla extract
6fl oz/175ml/¾ cup milk

For the filling

8fl oz/250ml/1 cup milk
3 egg yolks
90g/3½oz/½ cup caster
   (superfine) sugar
25g/1oz/¼ cup plain
   (all-purpose) flour
15ml/1 tbsp butter
5ml/1 tsp vanilla extract

For the chocolate glaze

25g/1oz dark (bittersweet)
   chocolate
15g/½oz/1 tbsp butter
50g/2oz/½ cup icing
   (confectioners') sugar, plus extra
   for dusting
2.5ml/½ tsp vanilla extract
15ml/1 tbsp hot water

1 Preheat the oven to 190°C/375°F/ Gas 5. Grease and line two 20cm/ 8in round shallow cake tins (pans) with baking parchment.

2 Sift the flour with the baking powder and salt into a large bowl.

3 In a large bowl, beat the butter and sugar together until light and fluffy. Beat in the eggs one at a time, beating well after each addition. Stir in the vanilla extract.

4 Add the milk and the dry ingredients, alternating the batches and mixing only enough to blend.

5 Divide the cake batter between the prepared tins and spread it out evenly.

6 Bake for 25 minutes, or until a skewer inserted into the centre comes out clean. Allow to stand in the tins for 5 minutes before turning out on to a wire rack to cool completely. Remove the lining.

7 To make the filling, heat the milk to boiling point in a small pan, and remove from the heat.

8 In a heatproof bowl, beat the egg yolks until smooth. Gradually add the sugar and continue beating until pale yellow, then beat in the flour.

9 While beating, pour the hot milk into the egg yolk mixture.

10 When all the milk has been added, put the bowl over a pan of boiling water. Heat, stirring constantly, until thickened. Cook for 2 minutes more, then remove from the heat.

11 Stir in the butter and vanilla extract. Leave to cool.

12 Slice off the domed top of each cake to create a flat surface, if necessary. Put one cake on a serving plate and spread on the filling in a thick layer. Set the other cake on top, cut side down. Smooth the edge of the filling layer so that it is flush with the sides of the cake layers.

13 To make the chocolate glaze, melt the chocolate and butter in a heatproof bowl set over a pan of gently simmering water. Stir well.

14 When smooth, remove from the heat and beat in the icing sugar using a wooden spoon. Add the vanilla extract, then beat in a little hot water to give a spreadable consistency. Spread evenly over the top of the cake. When it is set, dust the top with icing sugar.

Energy 499kcal/2100kJ; Protein 6g; Carbohydrate 77.1g, of which sugars 53.1g; Fat 20.3g, of which saturates 12.1g; Cholesterol 146mg; Calcium 112mg; Fibre 1g; Sodium 297mg.

Cinnamon meringues

These meringues have a hint of cinnamon and almond, which gives them a delicate flavour. They have a slightly chewy texture that goes particularly well with luscious summer fruits and amaretto-flavoured cream. Eat fresh, or store, undecorated, in an airtight container for two weeks.

MAKES 10

4 egg whites
1.25ml/¼ tsp cream of tartar
225g/8oz/generous 1 cup caster
　(superfine) sugar
2.5ml/½ tsp ground cinnamon
a few drops of almond extract
40g/1½oz/generous ⅓ cup
　ground almonds

For the filling
300ml/½ pint/1¼ cups double
　(heavy) cream
15ml/1 tbsp amaretto liqueur
　(optional)
350g/12oz/3 cups fresh redcurrants
　and raspberries
tiny sprigs of fresh mint

1 Preheat the oven to 110°C/225°F/Gas ¼. Line two baking sheets with baking parchment.

2 Rinse out a clean mixing bowl with boiling water, then dry with kitchen paper to make sure it is totally grease-free.

3 Put the egg whites into the bowl and whisk until they form stiff peaks. Add the cream of tartar. Gradually whisk in the sugar with the cinnamon and almond extract in small batches until the mixture is thick and stiff. Fold in the almonds.

COOK'S TIP
These cakes are not suitable for freezing.

4 Spoon 20 rough dessertspoonfuls on to the baking sheets, then bake for 2 hours, or until crisp and dry, swapping over the position of the baking sheets halfway through. Cool, then peel off from the papers.

5 Whip the cream until soft peaks form. Fold in the liqueur, if using, then fill a piping (pastry) bag. Pipe cream on to 10 meringue bases. Arrange the fruits, mint and meringue lid and serve immediately.

Energy 193kcal/821kJ; Protein 2.7g; Carbohydrate 40g, of which sugars 40g; Fat 1.6g, of which saturates 0.1g; Cholesterol 0mg; Calcium 31mg; Fibre 1.4g; Sodium 26mg.

Chocolate and strawberry-filled palmiers

Who could resist sweet and crisp puff pastry, with layers of chocolate, whipped cream and fresh strawberries, as a summer treat? These traditional little pastries, formed into rounded swirls, may look complicated but are actually easy to make, and they look delightful. Eat fresh.

MAKES 8

butter, for greasing
15g/½oz/2 tbsp unsweetened
  cocoa powder
375g/13oz puff pastry, thawed,
  if frozen
25g/1oz/2 tbsp golden caster
  (superfine) sugar

For the filling
300ml/½ pint/1¼ cups whipping
  cream, whipped
45ml/3 tbsp dark (bittersweet)
  chocolate spread
175g/6oz/generous 1 cup sliced
  strawberries
icing (confectioners') sugar,
  for dusting

1 Preheat the oven to 220°C/
425°F/Gas 7. Grease two large
baking sheets.

2 Dust a clean, dry working
surface lightly with 15ml/1 tbsp
cocoa powder.

3 Keeping the long side of pastry
towards you, roll it out on half the
cocoa powder to a rectangle 35 ×
23cm/14 × 9in. Lightly brush the
top of the pastry with cold water,
then sprinkle over the caster sugar
and remaining cocoa.

4 Measure and mark the centre of
the pastry. Roll up each of the short
sides like a Swiss roll (jelly roll) so
that they both meet in the centre.
Brush the join with a little water and
press the rolls together to secure.

5 Mark and then cut the roll into 16
slices. Arrange on the baking sheets,
spacing them well apart.

6 Bake for 8–10 minutes, or until
risen, puffy and golden brown.
Transfer to a wire rack to cool.

7 Lightly spread half the pastries
with the chocolate spread.

8 To make the filling, put the cream
in a piping (pastry) bag fitted with a
small plain nozzle. Pipe the cream
on top of the chocolate spread, then
top with a few strawberry slices.

9 Top each chocolate spread cream
and strawberry layer with a pastry.
Dust lightly with icing sugar and
serve immediately.

Energy 368kcal/1533kJ; Protein 4.2g; Carbohydrate 27g, of which sugars 9.7g; Fat 28.3g, of which saturates 10.4g; Cholesterol 40mg; Calcium 60mg; Fibre 0.5g; Sodium 180mg.

Indulgent Chocolate Cakes

Most people love chocolate, and this luxurious ingredient makes cakes rich and delectable. The flavour of chocolate varies according to the brand but, as a general rule, the higher the cocoa content, the better the quality. However, it is more important to find a chocolate that you enjoy. It is amazing how many ingredients work well with chocolate – who could resist juicy dark cherries with chocolate in Black Forest Gâteau or a sophisticated Chocolate Orange Marquise?

Chocolate potato cake

This very rich chocolate cake owes its moist texture to the addition of smooth mashed potato. Topped with chocolate fudge icing, the cake makes a superb dessert with a little whipped cream. Use a good-quality dark chocolate for the best results. This will keep for up to four days, chilled.

SERVES 10–12

225g/8oz/1 cup butter, plus extra
  for greasing
200g/7oz/1 cup caster
  (superfine) sugar
4 eggs, separated
175g/6oz dark (bittersweet)
  chocolate, finely grated
75g/3oz/¾ cup ground almonds
165g/5½oz/1½ cups
  mashed potato
225g/8oz/2 cup self-raising
  (self-rising) flour
5ml/1 tsp cinnamon
45ml/3 tbsp milk
chocolate curls, to decorate,
  see page 64
whipped cream, to serve

For the icing
115g/4oz dark (bittersweet)
  chocolate, broken into pieces
25g/1oz/2 tbsp butter, diced

1 Preheat the oven to 180°C/350°F/ Gas 4. Grease and line a 23cm/9in round deep cake tin (pan) with baking parchment.

2 In a large bowl, cream together the sugar and butter until fluffy.

3 Beat the egg yolks into the creamed mixture.

4 Stir the chocolate into the creamed mixture with the ground almonds.

5 Pass the mashed potato through a sieve (strainer) or ricer, and stir it into the creamed chocolate mixture.

6 Sift the flour and cinnamon and fold into the mixture with the milk.

7 Put the egg whites into a clean, grease-free bowl and whisk until stiff peaks form. Fold into the batter.

8 Turn into the prepared tin. Bake for 1¼ hours, or until a skewer inserted into the cake comes out clean.

9 Allow the cake to cool in the tin for 5 minutes. Turn out on to a wire rack to go cold. Peel off the paper.

10 To make the icing, melt the chocolate in a heatproof bowl over a pan of gently simmering water. Add the butter and stir until the mixture is smooth and glossy.

11 Smooth the icing over the cake. Decorate with white and dark chocolate shavings. Allow to set. Serve with whipped cream.

Energy 575kcal/2403kJ; Protein 8.7g; Carbohydrate 59g, of which sugars 39g; Fat 35.5g, of which saturates 18.8g; Cholesterol 146mg; Calcium 141mg; Fibre 2.1g; Sodium 273mg.

Chocolate brandy-snap gâteau

Savour every mouthful of this sensational dark chocolate gâteau. The cake is rich with chocolate and hazelnuts, then filled and topped with ganache – a cream and chocolate icing. Crisp brandy-snap frills look wonderful and contrast beautifully with the soft cake. Eat fresh.

SERVES 8

225g/8oz/1 cup unsalted butter, softened, plus extra for greasing
225g/8oz plain (semisweet) chocolate, broken into pieces
200g/7oz/scant 1 cup muscovado (molasses) sugar
6 eggs, separated
5ml/1 tsp vanilla extract
150g/5oz/1¼ cups ground hazelnuts
60ml/4 tbsp fresh white breadcrumbs
finely grated rind of 1 large orange
icing (confectioners') sugar, for dusting

For the brandy snaps
50g/2oz/¼ cup unsalted butter
50g/2oz/¼ cup caster (superfine) sugar
75g/3oz/¼ cup golden (light corn) syrup
50g/2oz/½ cup plain (all-purpose) flour
5ml/1 tsp brandy

For the chocolate ganache
250ml/8fl oz/1 cup double (heavy) cream
225g/8oz plain (semisweet) chocolate, broken into pieces

1 Preheat the oven to 180°C/250°F/Gas 4.

2 Grease and line two 20cm/8in round shallow cake tins (pans) and two baking sheets with baking parchment.

3 To make the cake, melt the chocolate in a heatproof bowl set over a pan of gently simmering water. Stir occasionally. Remove from the heat to cool slightly.

4 Beat the butter and sugar in a large bowl until pale and fluffy. Beat in the egg yolks and vanilla extract. Add the melted chocolate and mix thoroughly.

5 Put the egg whites into a clean, grease-free bowl and whisk until they form soft peaks.

6 Fold a tablespoon of the whites into the chocolate mixture to slacken it, then fold in the rest in batches with the ground hazelnuts, breadcrumbs and orange rind.

7 Divide the cake batter between the prepared tins and smooth the tops level.

8 Bake for 25–30 minutes, or until well risen and firm, then turn out to cool on wire racks. Remove the lining paper.

9 To make the brandy snaps, melt the butter, sugar and syrup in a pan over a low heat, stirring occasionally.

10 Remove from the heat and stir in the flour and brandy until smooth.

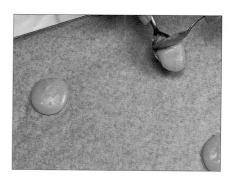

11 Place small spoonfuls well apart on the baking sheet leaving enough space to allow each biscuit to spread out, and bake for 10–15 minutes, or until golden.

Energy 870kcal/3622kJ; Protein 10.7g; Carbohydrate 70g, of which sugars 59g; Fat 62.7g, of which saturates 31.2g; Cholesterol 244mg; Calcium 102mg; Fibre 2.3g; Sodium 424mg.

12 Cool for a few seconds until firm enough to lift.

13 Immediately pinch the edges of each brandy snap to make a frilled effect. If the biscuits become too firm, pop them back into the oven for a few minutes. Leave to set on a wire rack.

14 Meanwhile, to make the chocolate ganache, heat the cream and chocolate together in a pan over a low heat, stirring frequently until the chocolate has melted.

15 Pour into a bowl. Leave to cool, then stir until the mixture begins to hold its shape.

16 Sandwich the cake layers together with half the chocolate ganache, transfer to a plate and spread the remaining ganache on top.

17 Arrange the brandy snap frills over the gâteau and dust with icing sugar. Serve immediately.

Frosted chocolate fudge cake

Rich and dreamy, this chocolate cake has added depth of flavour from muscovado sugar and thick yogurt. The chocolate fudge frosting also contains yogurt, giving it a creamy consistency. It couldn't be easier to make, or more delicious to eat. Keep, refrigerated, for up to three days.

SERVES 8

175g/6oz/¾ cup unsalted butter, softened, plus extra for greasing
115g/4oz plain (semisweet) chocolate, broken into pieces
200g/7oz/scant 1 cup light muscovado (brown) sugar
5ml/1 tsp vanilla extract
3 eggs, beaten
150ml/¼ pint/⅔ cup Greek (US strained plain) yogurt
150g/5oz/1¼ cups self-raising (self-rising) flour

For the frosting and chocolate curls
2255g/8oz plain (semisweet) chocolate, broken into pieces
50g/2oz/¼ cup unsalted butter
90ml/6 tbsp Greek (US strained plain) yogurt
350g/12oz/3 cups icing (confectioners') sugar, plus extra for dusting

1 Preheat the oven to 190°C/375°F/Gas 5. Grease and line two 20cm/8in round shallow cake tins (pans) with baking parchment.

2 Melt the chocolate in a heatproof bowl over a pan of simmering water.

3 Meanwhile, in a large bowl, beat the butter with the sugar until light and fluffy.

4 Beat in the vanilla extract, then gradually beat in the egg in small quantities, beating well after each addition.

5 Stir in the melted chocolate and yogurt. Sift the flour over the mixture, then fold in gently with a large metal spoon.

6 Divide the mixture between the tins. Bake for 25–30 minutes, or until the cakes are firm to the touch.

7 Leave to stand for 5 minutes, then turn out on to a wire rack to go cold. Remove the lining papers.

8 To make the chocolate curls, melt 115g/4oz of the chocolate in a heatproof bowl set over a pan of gently simmering water.

9 Spread the melted chocolate out on to a clean, cold hard surface, preferably marble, and allow to set.

10 Meanwhile, to make the frosting, melt the rest of the chocolate and all the butter in a medium pan over a gentle heat.

11 Stir in the yogurt and icing sugar. Mix with a rubber spatula until smooth, then beat until the frosting begins to cool and thicken slightly.

12 Use a third of the mixture to sandwich the cakes together. Working quickly, spread the rest of the frosting over the top and sides.

13 To make the curls, using a long, sharp knife, scrape along the surface of the set chocolate to make thin curled shavings.

14 Position the shavings on the cake and then dust with icing sugar.

Energy 753kcal/3160kJ; Protein 8g; Carbohydrate 105.4g, of which sugars 90.9g; Fat 36.6g, of which saturates 21.7g; Cholesterol 133mg; Calcium 133mg; Fibre 1.3g; Sodium 224mg.

Devilish chocolate roulade with mascarpone

This decadent roulade can be made a day ahead and then filled and rolled before serving. It has a rich brandy, chocolate and mascarpone filling and is decorated with chocolate-dipped strawberries to make it extra special. Once filled, keep it, refrigerated, for up to two days.

SERVES 6–8

butter, for greasing
175g/6oz plain (semisweet)
   chocolate, broken into pieces
4 eggs, separated
115g/4oz/generous ½ cup caster
   (superfine) sugar
unsweetened cocoa powder,
   for dusting

For the filling
225g/8oz plain (semisweet)
   chocolate, broken into pieces
45ml/3 tbsp brandy
2 eggs, separated
250g/9oz/generous 1 cup
   mascarpone
chocolate-dipped strawberries

1 Preheat the oven to 180°C/350°F/ Gas 4. Grease and line a 33 × 23cm/ 13 × 9in Swiss roll tin (jelly roll pan) with baking parchment.

2 Melt the chocolate in a heatproof bowl over a pan of gently simmering water, then remove from the heat.

3 Whisk the egg yolks and sugar in a bowl until pale and thick, then stir in the melted chocolate.

4 Put the egg whites into a clean, grease-free bowl and whisk until they form soft peaks, then fold lightly and evenly into the egg and chocolate mixture.

5 Pour the mixture into the prepared tin and smooth level. Bake for 15–20 minutes, or until well risen and firm to the touch.

6 Dust a sheet of baking parchment with cocoa. Turn the sponge out on to the paper, cover with a clean dish towel and leave to cool.

7 To make the filling, melt the chocolate with the brandy in a heatproof bowl set over a pan of gently simmering water. Remove from the heat.

8 Beat the egg yolks together, then beat into the warm chocolate mixture until smooth.

9 Put the egg whites into a clean, grease-free bowl and whisk until they form soft peaks. Fold them lightly and evenly into the filling in three batches until the mixture is light and smooth. Cool completely.

10 Uncover the roulade, remove the lining paper and spread with most of the mascarpone.

11 Spread the chocolate mixture over the top, then roll up from a long side to enclose the filling.

12 Transfer to a serving plate, top with mascarpone, fresh chocolate-dipped strawberries, and dust with cocoa powder.

CHOCOLATE-DIPPED STRAWBERRIES
Dip the lower half of each strawberry into some good quality melted chocolate. Leave to set on a baking sheet lined with baking parchment.

Energy 486kcal/2022kJ; Protein 10.2g; Carbohydrate 32.8g, of which sugars 32.4g; Fat 34.5g, of which saturates 19.9g; Cholesterol 189mg; Calcium 41mg; Fibre 1.3g; Sodium 143mg.

Black Forest gâteau

Perhaps the most famous chocolate cake of all, this Kirsch-flavoured gâteau is layered with fresh cream containing chopped black cherries, and is decorated with chocolate curls. It is the perfect gâteau for a special-occasion dessert. This will keep, refrigerated, for up to three days.

SERVES 10–12

75g/3oz/6 tbsp butter, melted,
  plus extra for greasing
5 eggs
175g/6oz/scant 1 cup caster
  (superfine) sugar
50g/2oz/½ cup plain (all-purpose)
  flour, sifted
50g/2oz/½ cup unsweetened cocoa
  powder, sifted

For the filling and topping
75–90ml/5–6 tbsp Kirsch
600ml/1 pint/2½ cups double
  (heavy) cream
425g/15oz can black cherries,
  drained, pitted and chopped

For the decoration
225g/8oz plain (semisweet)
  chocolate, to make chocolate
  curls, *see page 64*
15–20 fresh cherries, preferably
  with stems
sifted icing (confectioners')
  sugar (optional)

1 Preheat the oven to 180°C/350°F/ Gas 4. Grease and line two 20cm/ 8in round deep cake tins (pans) with baking parchment.

2 Put the eggs and sugar in a large bowl and beat with an electric whisk for about 10 minutes, or until the mixture is thick and pale and leaves a trail when the beaters are lifted.

3 Sift together the flour and cocoa powder, then sift again into the whisked mixture. Fold in gently using a metal spoon and a figure-of-eight motion.

4 Slowly trickle in the cooled melted butter and fold in gently.

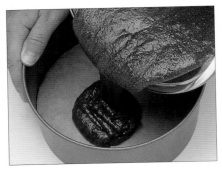

5 Divide the batter between the tins and smooth level. Bake for 30 minutes, until springy to the touch.

6 Leave in the tin for 5 minutes, then turn out on to a wire rack to cool. Peel off the lining paper.

7 Cut each cake in half horizontally. Sprinkle the four layers evenly with the Kirsch.

8 In a large bowl, whip the cream until it holds soft peaks.

9 Transfer two-thirds of the cream to another bowl and stir in the chopped cherries.

10 Place a layer of cake on a serving plate and spread over one-third of the filling. Top with another portion of cake and continue layering, finishing with the cake top.

11 Use the remaining whipped cream to cover the top and sides of the gâteau. Decorate with chocolate curls, cherries and a dusting of icing sugar.

Energy 448kcal/1864kJ; Protein 4.8g; Carbohydrate 26.4g, of which sugars 22.7g; Fat 35.2g, of which saturates 21.1g; Cholesterol 161mg; Calcium 61.8mg; Fibre 0.8g; Sodium 121mg.

Chocolate gooey cake

For perfect results it is essential to undercook this cake so that it is soft in the middle, so it is unsuitable for children and the elderly. It is made with almonds instead of flour, and so has a superb nutty flavour and is also gluten-free. Serve as a dessert with whipped cream. Eat fresh.

SERVES 8

115g/4oz/½ cup unsalted butter,
  diced, plus extra for greasing
115g/4oz dark (bittersweet)
  chocolate, broken into pieces
2 eggs, separated
175g/6oz/1½ cups ground almonds
5ml/1 tsp vanilla sugar
whipped double (heavy) cream,
  to serve

1 Preheat the oven to 180°C/350°F/ Gas 4. Grease and line a 20cm/8in round shallow cake tin (pan).

2 Put the chocolate into a pan. Add 5ml/1 tsp water and heat very gently until the chocolate has melted, stirring occasionally. Remove from the heat.

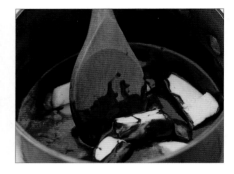

3 Add the butter to the chocolate and stir until melted.

4 Add the egg yolks, ground almonds and vanilla sugar, and stir together. Turn the mixture into a large bowl.

5 Put the egg whites into a clean, grease-free bowl and whisk until they form stiff peaks, then fold in batches into the chocolate mixture.

6 Put the mixture into the prepared tin and bake for 15–17 minutes, or until just set. The mixture should still be soft in the centre.

7 Leave to cool in the tin, then carefully turn out on to a serving plate. Remove the lining paper. Serve with whipped cream.

Energy 311kcal/1288kJ; Protein 6.8g; Carbohydrate 10g, of which sugars 9.3g; Fat 27.4g, of which saturates 9.9g; Cholesterol 75mg; Calcium 66.2mg; Fibre 1.9g; Sodium 97mg.

Devil's food cake

Originating in the US and dating back to 1905, this cake is always made using cocoa powder rather than melted chocolate. The chocolate cake is layered and covered with a fine white frosting flavoured with orange. It tastes very good indeed, and will keep for four days.

SERVES 10–12

175g/6oz/³⁄₄ cup butter, at room
    temperature, plus extra
    for greasing
50g/2oz/¹⁄₂ cup unsweetened
    cocoa powder
350g/12oz/scant 2 cups soft dark
    brown sugar
3 eggs
275g/10oz/1¹⁄₂ cups plain
    (all-purpose) flour
7.5ml/1¹⁄₂ tsp bicarbonate of soda
    (baking soda)
1.5ml/¹⁄₄ tsp baking powder
120ml/4fl oz/¹⁄₂ cup sour cream
shreds of orange rind, to decorate

For the frosting
300g/11oz/1¹⁄₂ cups caster
    (superfine) sugar
2 egg whites
60ml/4 tbsp orange juice
    concentrate
15ml/1 tbsp lemon juice
grated rind of 1 orange

1 Preheat the oven to 180°C/350°F/ Gas 4. Grease and line two 23cm/9in round shallow cake tins (pans) with baking parchment.

2 In a bowl, mix the cocoa powder with 175ml/6fl oz/³⁄₄ cup boiling water until smooth. Leave to cool.

3 Beat the butter and sugar until light and fluffy, then beat in the eggs one at a time.

4 When the cocoa mixture is luke-warm, add it to the butter mixture.

5 Sift the flour, bicarbonate of soda and baking powder into the cocoa mixture in three batches, alternating with the soured cream.

6 Pour into the tins and bake for 30–35 minutes, or until the cake pulls away from the sides.

7 Leave to cool in the tins for 15 minutes, then turn out to cool on a wire rack to go cold. Remove the lining papers.

8 To make the frosting, put all the ingredients into a heatproof bowl set over a pan of gently simmering water. With an electric whisk, beat until the mixture holds soft peaks. Remove from the heat and continue beating until thick enough to spread.

9 Quickly sandwich the cake layers with frosting, then spread over the top and sides. Decorate with orange rind shreds.

Energy 455kcal/1916kJ; Protein 5.7g; Carbohydrate 75.5g, of which sugars 57.6g; Fat 16.6g, of which saturates 9.6g; Cholesterol 84.6mg; Calcium 86.5mg; Fibre 1.2g; Sodium 165mg.

Chocolate drizzle cake

Make this moist chocolate and hazelnut cake to please all the family. The decoration couldn't be simpler, but it looks effective. The cake is easy to make, children and adults love it, and it can even be served with fresh summer fruits or a scoop of ice cream.

SERVES 10

115g/4oz/½ cup butter, softened,
  plus extra for greasing
175g/6oz/scant 1 cup natural caster
  (superfine) sugar
4 large (US extra large) eggs,
  separated
175g/6oz/1½ cups self-raising
  (self-rising) flour, sifted
115g/4oz plain (semisweet)
  chocolate, grated
90ml/6 tbsp milk
115g/4oz/1 cup ground hazelnuts

For the filling and topping
60ml/4 tbsp chocolate and
  hazelnut spread, warmed
200g/7oz milk chocolate
150g/5oz white chocolate
edible gold or silver balls
Materials: wired silver ribbon

1 Preheat the oven to 220°C/
425°F/Gas 7. Grease and line a
20cm/8in deep round cake tin (pan)
with baking parchment.

2 Beat the butter and sugar
together until light and fluffy, then
whisk in the egg yolks gradually,
adding 5ml/1 tsp flour with each
addition to prevent the mixture
from curdling.

COOK'S TIP
The cake keeps for 4 days in an
airtight container. Freeze the
base, undecorated and wrapped
in foil, for up to 2 months.

3 Fold in the grated chocolate, milk
and ground hazelnuts until smooth.

4 Whisk the egg whites in a clean,
grease-free bowl until they form soft
peaks. Fold them into the mixture,
alternating with the remaining flour.

5 Spoon into the tin and smooth
level. Reduce the oven temperature
to 170C/350F/Gas 3. Bake in the
centre of the oven for about 1 hour
10 minutes, or until the centre
springs back when pressed.

6 Cool in the tin for 5 minutes, then
turn out to cool on a wire rack and
peel away the lining paper.

7 Cut the cake in half, and cover
one half with warmed chocolate
spread.

8 Sandwich the other half on top
and put them on to a serving plate.

9 Melt the chocolates in two
separate heatproof bowls set over
pans of gently simmering water,
then spoon into two separate small
paper piping (pastry) bags.
Alternatively, melt in two heatproof
bowls in the microwave oven.

10 Snip off the end of each bag and
drizzle each chocolate over the top
and side of the cake in a
random pattern.

11 Sprinkle the edible gold or
silver balls over the top and leave
to set for 1 hour. Finish with a large
wired bow in the centre of the cake,
or add candles if made for a
birthday celebration.

Energy 430kcal/1790kJ; Protein 7.8g; Carbohydrate 29.5g, of which sugars 28.8g; Fat 32.1g, of which saturates 13.6g; Cholesterol 96mg; Calcium 92mg; Fibre 1.9g; Sodium 125mg.

Chocolate orange marquise

This fabulous cake has very little flour, but is rich with butter, eggs and chocolate, and flavoured with orange rind and juice. Enjoy this special cake with cream as a dessert – it is rich enough to serve at a dinner party. Store chilled in an airtight container for up to three days.

SERVES 6–8

225g/8oz/1 cup unsalted butter,
   diced, at room temperature, plus
   extra for greasing
200g/7oz/1 cup caster
   (superfine) sugar
60ml/4 tbsp freshly squeezed
   orange juice
350g/12oz plain (semisweet)
   chocolate, broken into pieces
5 eggs
finely grated rind of 1 orange
45ml/3 tbsp plain
   (all-purpose) flour
icing (confectioners') sugar,
   to decorate
finely pared strips of orange rind,
   to decorate

1 Preheat the oven to 180°C/350°F/ Gas 4. Grease and line a 23cm/9in round deep cake tin (pan) with baking parchment.

2 Put 115g/4oz/generous ½ cup of the caster sugar in a heavy pan with the fresh orange juice. Place over a low heat until all the sugar has dissolved. Stir constantly so that the sugar does not catch and burn. Do not allow to boil.

3 Remove from the heat and stir in the chocolate until melted, then add the butter, stirring, until melted and evenly mixed. Cool.

4 Put the eggs with the remaining sugar in a large bowl and whisk until pale and very thick. Add the orange rind.

5 Using a metal spoon, fold the chocolate mixture lightly and evenly into the egg mixture using a metal spoon and a figure-of-eight motion. Sift the flour over and fold in evenly.

COOK'S TIP
Make the marquise ahead of time and freeze for up to 3 months in a freezerproof box.

6 Scrape the mixture into the prepared tin. Put the tin into a roasting pan, then pour hot water into the roasting pan to reach half-way up the outside of the cake tin.

7 Bake for 1 hour, or until the cake is firm to the touch. Carefully remove the cake tin from the roasting pan and cool for 15–20 minutes.

8 Invert the cake on a baking sheet. Lift away the tin and lining paper. Place a serving plate over the cake, then turn the baking sheet and plate over as one so that the cake is transferred to the plate.

9 Dust with icing sugar, decorate with strips of pared orange rind and serve slightly warm or cold.

Energy 553kcal/2309kJ; Protein 3.1g; Carbohydrate 59.1g, of which sugars 54.4g; Fat 35.5g, of which saturates 22g; Cholesterol 63mg; Calcium 41mg; Fibre 1.3g; Sodium 176mg.

Sachertorte

This glorious gâteau has a pedigree going back to 1832, when it was created by Franz Sacher, a chef of the royal household in Vienna. It is rich and dark, with a flavour that contrasts with the apricot glaze – and it is topped with a rich, glossy icing. Keep, refrigerated, for up to three days.

SERVES 10–12

150g/5oz/10 tbsp unsalted butter, plus extra for greasing
115g/4oz/generous ½ cup caster (superfine) sugar
8 eggs, separated
225g/8oz dark (bittersweet) chocolate, melted and cooled
115g/4oz/1 cup plain (all-purpose) flour

For the glaze
225g/8oz/1 cup apricot jam
15ml/1 tbsp lemon juice

For the icing
225g/8oz dark (bittersweet) chocolate, broken into pieces
200g/7oz/1 cup caster (superfine) sugar
15ml/1 tbsp golden (light corn) syrup
250ml/8fl oz/1 cup double (heavy) cream
5ml/1 tsp vanilla extract
chocolate curls, to decorate, *see page 64*

1 Preheat the oven to 180°C/350°F/ Gas 4. Grease and line a 23cm/9in round deep cake tin (pan).

2 In a bowl, beat the butter with the sugar until pale and fluffy, then add the egg yolks, one at a time, beating well after each addition.

3 Beat in the melted chocolate, then sift the flour over the mixture and fold it in evenly with a large metal spoon.

4 Put the egg whites into a clean, grease-free bowl and whisk until they form stiff peaks.

5 Stir about a quarter of the whites into the chocolate mixture to lighten it, then fold in the remaining whites.

6 Pour the mixture into the prepared tin and smooth the top level. Bake for 50–55 minutes, or until firm.

7 Leave to stand in the tin for 5 minutes, then turn out on to a wire rack to go cold. Remove the lining paper. Slice in half across the middle to make two even layers.

8 To make the glaze, heat the apricot jam with the lemon juice in a small pan until melted, then strain through a sieve (strainer) into a bowl.

9 Brush the top and sides of each layer with the apricot glaze, then sandwich them together. Put the cake on a wire rack.

10 To make the icing, put the chocolate, sugar, golden syrup, cream and vanilla extract in a pan. Heat gently, stirring constantly, until the mixture is thick and smooth.

11 Simmer gently for 3–4 minutes, without stirring, until the mixture registers 95°C/200°F on a sugar thermometer.

12 Pour the icing quickly over the cake, spreading to cover the top and sides completely.

13 Leave to set, then decorate with chocolate curls.

Energy 625kcal/2618kJ; Protein 7.6g; Carbohydrate 73.1g, of which sugars 65.5g; Fat 35.8g, of which saturates 20.8g; Cholesterol 184mg; Calcium 73mg; Fibre 1.2g; Sodium 143mg.

Iced Cakes, Cheesecakes and Showstoppers

In this chapter you will find some fabulous cakes to celebrate special occasions, such as birthdays and family gatherings, all of which call for a centrepiece. Give yourself plenty of time to make these cakes; the detailed step-by-step photographs will guide you through the techniques.

Cheesecakes are a favourite dinner party dessert that can be made in advance. You have plenty of choice here: delicious Polish Cheesecake, Rum and Raisin Cheesecake and Baked Coffee Cheesecake.

Iced raspberry pavlova roulade

This melt-in-the-mouth meringue, rolled around vanilla cream and luscious raspberries, is a star dinner-party attraction, and is surprisingly quick and simple to make. Eat it fresh, or store it in the freezer in a rigid plastic container. Keep frozen for up to three months, and defrost for four hours.

SERVES 6–8

10ml/2 tsp cornflour (cornstarch)
225g/8oz/generous 1 cup caster
  (superfine) sugar
4 egg whites, at room temperature
icing (confectioners') sugar, sifted,
  for dusting
300ml/½ pint/1¼ cups double
  (heavy) cream or whipping cream
a few drops of vanilla extract
175g/6oz/1 cup raspberries, partly
  frozen, plus extra to serve

1 Line a 33 x 23cm/13 x 9in Swiss roll tin (jelly roll pan) with baking parchment.

2 Sift the cornflour into a bowl and blend evenly with the sugar.

3 Put the egg whites into a clean, grease-free bowl and whisk until stiff peaks form.

4 Whisk in the caster sugar, a few spoonfuls at a time, until the mixture becomes stiff and glossy.

VARIATIONS
• Flavour the cream with liqueur or lemon curd.
• Fill with soft ice cream.

5 Spoon the mixture into the prepared tin and smooth it level.

6 Put the meringue into a cold oven and turn the temperature to 150°C/300°F/Gas 2. Bake for 1 hour, or until the top is crisp and the meringue feels springy.

7 Turn out on to baking parchment sprinkled with sifted icing sugar, and leave to go cold.

8 Meanwhile, whip the cream and vanilla. Stir in the raspberries.

9 Spread the raspberry cream over the meringue, then roll up, using the paper as a support. Freeze for 1 hour before serving. Dust with icing sugar and top with more raspberries, to serve.

Energy 243kcal/1015kJ; Protein 2g; Carbohydrate 26g, of which sugars 26g; Fat 15.3g, of which saturates 9.5g; Cholesterol 39mg; Calcium 34mg; Fibre 0.5g; Sodium 33mg.

Raspberry mousse cake

A lavish amount of raspberries gives this freezer gâteau its vibrant colour and flavour. Make it at the height of summer when these deliciously scented fruits are plentiful and their flavour is at its best. Keep this cake frozen for three months. Thaw it in the refrigerator.

SERVES 8–10

2 eggs
50g/2oz/¼ cup sugar
50g/2oz/½ cup plain
 (all-purpose) flour
30ml/2 tbsp unsweetened
 cocoa powder
600g/1lb 5oz/3½ cups raspberries
115g/4oz 1 cup icing
 (confectioners') sugar
300ml/½ pint/1¼ cups
 whipping cream
2 egg whites

1 Preheat the oven to 180°C/350°F/ Gas 4. Grease and line a 23cm/9in round cake tin (pan).

2 Whisk the eggs and sugar in a bowl set over a pan of simmering water until the beaters leave a trail when lifted. Remove from the heat.

3 Sift over the flour and cocoa and fold it in with a metal spoon. Spoon into the tin. Bake for 12–15 minutes, or until just firm. Turn out to cool on a wire rack.

4 Reline the tin with baking paper and replace the cake. Freeze.

5 Set aside 175g/6oz/1 cup of raspberries.

6 Put the rest of the raspberries in a a food processor bowl, stir in the icing sugar and process to a purée.

7 Whip the cream to form soft peaks.

8 Put the egg whites into a clean, grease-free bowl and whisk until they form stiff peaks.

9 Using a large metal spoon, fold the cream, then the egg whites into the raspberry purée.

10 Spread half the raspberry mixture on to the cake. Sprinkle with the reserved raspberries. Spread the remaining raspberry mixture on top. Freeze overnight, then thaw for at least 2 hours before serving.

Energy 238kcal/996kJ; Protein 4.4g; Carbohydrate 25g, of which sugars 20.9g; Fat 14.1g, of which saturates 8.3g; Cholesterol 70mg; Calcium 58mg; Fibre 2g; Sodium 65mg.

Polish cheesecake

There are many different versions of cheesecake. Unlike others, this rich, creamy baked version is not made on a biscuit base, but includes raisins and semolina, giving it sweetness and a firm texture. Keep this cheesecake refrigerated for two days, and freeze for up to two months.

SERVES 6–8

100g/3¾oz/scant ½ cup butter, softened, plus extra for greasing
500g/1¼lb/2¼ cups curd cheese
2.5ml/½ tsp vanilla extract
6 eggs, separated
150g/5½oz/scant ¾ cup caster (superfine) sugar
10ml/2 tsp grated lemon rind
15ml/1 tbsp cornflour (cornstarch)
15ml/1 tbsp semolina
50g/2oz/⅓ cup raisins
icing (confectioners') sugar, for dusting

1 Preheat the oven to 200°C/400°F/ Gas 6. Grease and line the base and sides of a 20cm/8in loose-based cake tin (pan) with baking parchment.

2 In a large bowl, cream together the curd cheese, butter and vanilla extract.

3 Put the egg whites into a clean, grease-free bowl and add 15ml/ 1 tbsp sugar. Whisk until the whites form stiff peaks.

4 Whisk the egg yolks with the remaining sugar until thick and creamy. Add to the cheese mixture with the lemon rind, and stir to combine.

5 Gently fold in the egg whites, then fold in the cornflour, semolina and raisins.

6 Transfer to the lined tin and bake for 1 hour, or until the cake is set and golden brown.

7 Leave to cool in the tin. Remove the sides of the tin and papers, then dust with icing sugar and serve.

Energy 347kcal/1488kJ; Protein 10.8g; Carbohydrate 24.8g, of which sugars 21.6g; Fat23.6g, of which saturates 13.4g; Cholesterol 196mg; Calcium 34mg; Fibre 0g; Sodium131mg.

Baked coffee cheesecake

This rich, baked and chilled cheesecake, flavoured with coffee and orange liqueur, has a wonderfully dense, velvety texture and makes a lovely dessert served with single cream. Keep for two days refrigerated. Freeze for up to two months.

SERVES 8

75g/3oz/6 tbsp butter, plus extra
   for greasing
115g/4oz/1 cup plain
   (all-purpose) flour
5ml/1 tsp baking powder
50g/2oz/¼ cup caster
   (superfine) sugar
1 egg, lightly beaten
30ml/2 tbsp cold water
single (light) cream, to serve

For the filling
45ml/3 tbsp near-boiling water
30ml/2 tbsp ground coffee
4 eggs
225g/8oz/generous 1 cup caster
   (superfine) sugar
450g/1lb/2 cups cream cheese, at
   room temperature
30ml/2 tbsp orange liqueur
40g/1½ oz/⅓ cup plain
   (all-purpose) flour, sifted
300ml/½ pint/1¼ cups
   whipping cream
30ml/2 tbsp icing (confectioners')
   sugar, for dusting

1 Preheat the oven to 160°C/325°F/ Gas 3. Grease and line a 20cm/8in round loose-based cake tin (pan) with baking parchment.

2 Sift the flour and baking powder into a bowl. Rub in the butter until the mixture resembles fine crumbs.

3 Stir in the sugar, then add the egg and the cold water, and mix to a dough. Press the mixture into the base of the tin.

4 For the filling, pour the water over the coffee and leave for 4 minutes. Strain through a fine sieve (strainer).

5 Whisk the eggs and sugar until thick.

6 Using a wooden spoon, beat the cream cheese until softened, then beat in the liqueur, a spoonful at a time.

7 Gradually mix in the whisked eggs. Fold in the flour. Finally, stir in the whipping cream and coffee.

8 Pour over the base and bake for 1½ hours. Turn off the heat. Leave in the oven to go cold with the door ajar.

9 Chill for 1 hour. Remove from the tin and dust with icing sugar.

Energy 713kcal/2969kJ; Protein 8.4g; Carbohydrate 53.4g, of which sugars 38.6g; Fat 52.8g, of which saturates 32g; Cholesterol 233mg; Calcium 143mg; Fibre 0.6g; Sodium 301mg.

Rum and raisin cheesecake

Spectacular to look at, and superb to eat, this light, rum-flavoured cheesecake is studded with raisins and surrounded by diagonal stripes of plain and chocolate sponge. Keep this for four days refrigerated in an airtight container, or freeze for up to two months, undecorated with cream.

SERVES 8–10

115g/4oz/½ cup unsalted butter,
   melted, plus extra for greasing
2 eggs
50g/2oz/¼ cup caster
   (superfine) sugar
50g/2oz/½ cup plain (all-purpose)
   flour, sifted
5ml/1 tsp unsweetened cocoa
   powder, mixed to a paste with
   15ml/1 tbsp hot water and cooled
225g/8oz ginger biscuits
   (gingersnaps), crushed
whipped cream and sifted
   unsweetened cocoa powder,
   to decorate

For the filling
45ml/3 tbsp water
1 sachet powdered gelatine
300ml/½ pint/1¼ cups double
   (heavy) cream
30ml/2 tbsp milk
75g/3oz/generous ½ cup raisins
60ml/4 tbsp rum
50g/2oz/½ cup icing
   (confectioners') sugar, sifted
450g/1lb/2 cups curd cheese

1 Preheat the oven to 200°C/400°F/
Gas 6. Grease and line a 28 x 18cm/
11 x 7in Swiss roll tin (jelly roll pan)
with baking parchment. Also, grease
and line a 20cm/8in round loose-
based cake tin (pan). Cover a wire
rack with baking parchment.

2 Mix the eggs and sugar in a
heatproof bowl. Put over a pan of
barely simmering water and whisk
until the mixture forms a thick trail.

3 Fold in the sifted flour using a
metal spoon.

4 Spoon half the mixture into a large
piping bag fitted with a 4cm/1½in
star nozzle, or use a paper piping
(pastry) bag and cut the end off.
Pipe diagonal stripes of the cake
mixture across the tin, leaving an
equal space between each row.

5 Stir the cooled cocoa paste into
the remaining cake mixture until
evenly mixed. Fill a piping bag
with the batter and pipe as before,
filling the gaps to give rows of
alternating colours.

6 Bake for 10–12 minutes, then
turn out the sponge on to the paper-
topped wire rack. Peel off the
lining paper. Leave to go cold.

7 Mix the melted butter and crushed
ginger biscuits in a bowl. Spread
over the bottom of the cake tin and
press down firmly.

8 Cut the sponge in half lengthways
and arrange the two strips around
the sides of the cake tin. Set aside.

9 To make the filling, put the water
into a small heatproof bowl and
sprinkle over the gelatine. Leave
until spongy. Put the bowl over a
pan of barely simmering water and
stir until the gelatine dissolves.
Remove from the heat and leave to
cool slightly.

10 Whisk the cream with the milk
in a bowl. Fold in the raisins, rum,
icing sugar and curd cheese, then
stir in the cooled gelatine.

11 Spoon the filling into the
prepared tin and chill until set.

12 To serve, carefully remove the
cheesecake from the tin and place
on a serving plate. Trim the cake
level with the filling. Dust with
cocoa powder and pipe whirls of
cream around the edge.

Energy 467kcal/1946kJ; Protein 10.5g; Carbohydrate 34.6g, of which sugars 21.1g; Fat 33.3g, of which saturates 19.5g; Cholesterol 114mg; Calcium 121mg; Fibre 0.6g; Sodium 389mg.

Cassata

This traditional cake from Sicily has a rich and sweet filling of honey, Marsala and ricotta cheese studded with candied peel and chocolate chips. The cake is covered with almond paste and decorated with jewel-like glacé fruits. It is stunning to look at, and very tasty indeed.

SERVES 12

butter, for greasing
4 eggs
115g/4oz/generous ½ cup caster
  (superfine) sugar
115g/4oz/1 cup plain
  (all-purpose) flour
100ml/3½fl oz/scant ½ cup
  Marsala wine

For the filling
350g/12oz/1½ cups ricotta cheese
  30ml/2 tbsp clear honey
15ml/1 tbsp Marsala wine
1.5ml/¼ tsp vanilla extract
grated rind and juice of ½ lemon
115g/4oz/⅔ cup mixed (candied)
  peel, finely chopped
75g/3oz/½ cup plain (semisweet)
  chocolate chips

For the icing
175g/6oz/1½ cups ground
  almonds
75g/3oz/6 tbsp caster
  (superfine) sugar
75g/3oz/¾ cup icing
  (confectioners') sugar, sifted,
  plus extra for dusting
1 egg white, lightly beaten
5ml/1 tsp lemon juice
2 drops almond extract
green food colouring, optional
45ml/3 tbsp apricot jam, warmed
225g/8oz/mixed glacé
  (candied) fruits

1 Preheat the oven to 180°C/
350°F/Gas 4. Grease and line a
23cm/9in round cake tin (pan) with
baking parchment.

2 Line a 20cm/8in round cake tin
(pan) with clear film (plastic wrap).

3 Whisk the eggs and sugar in a
heatproof bowl until blended. Put
the bowl over a pan of simmering
water and whisk until thick and
pale. Remove from the heat and
continue whisking until the mixture
is cool and leaves a thick trail on the
surface when the beaters are lifted.

4 Sift the flour into the egg mixture.
Using a plastic spatula, fold the flour
into the beaten egg until smooth.

5 Pour into the larger prepared tin,
and bake for 30 minutes, or until
firm and spongy to the touch. Leave
to set in the tin for 10 minutes, then
turn out to go cold on a wire rack.
Peel away the lining papers.

6 Cut the cake into three layers.
Trim one to fit the base of the
smaller tin. Cut the second into
strips to line the tin side. Brush with
some of the Marsala. Reserve the
trimmings and the last sponge layer.

7 To make the filling, beat the
ricotta, honey, 15ml/1 tbsp Marsala,
vanilla extract and lemon rind and
juice together until very smooth.

8 Chop the sponge trimmings and
stir into the cheese mixture, with the
peel and chocolate chips. Spoon into
the sponge case, pressing into place.

COOK'S TIP
Marsala is a delicious golden
fortified dessert wine from Sicily.

Energy 380kcal/1599kJ; Protein 9.3g; Carbohydrate 50.8g, of which sugars 43.8g; Fat 13.3g, of which saturates 7.3g; Cholesterol 97mg; Calcium 72mg; Fibre 1.9g; Sodium 115mg.

9 Trim the reserved layer of sponge cake to fit tightly over the filling. Pour over the remaining Marsala and cover with clear film. Place a weight on top of the cake and chill for several hours, until firm.

10 To make the icing, combine the almonds, caster sugar and icing sugar in a bowl. Make a well in the centre.

11 Pour in the egg white, lemon juice and almond extract, and work in to form a soft pliable paste. Add a few drops of food colouring, if you like.

12 Knead the icing on a clean surface, dusted with a little icing sugar, until smooth and evenly coloured. Wrap and keep cool until required.

13 Remove the cake from the refrigerator and turn out of the tin. Remove the clear film and brush the cake with warmed apricot jam.

14 Roll out the almond paste to a circle a little larger than the cake and use to cover, pressing gently to the top and sides. Smooth over the icing with a metal spatula or lightly with a rolling pin. Transfer to a cake plate.

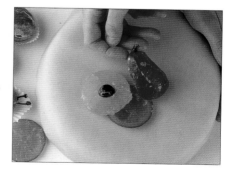

15 Make an attractive arrangement of mixed glacé fruits in the centre of the cake. Keep chilled until ready to serve. Serve with whipped cream. It will keep refrigerated, in an airtight container for 3 days.

Princess cake

A light sponge cake is layered and topped with vanilla custard cream, then covered with home-made marzipan to make an unusual and special dessert gâteau. You can make the marzipan in advance, if you like. Serve a slice of the cake with strawberries. Keep for two days in a cool place.

SERVES 8–10

200g/7oz/scant 1 cup unsalted
   butter, plus extra for greasing
400g/14oz/2 cups caster
   (superfine) sugar
3 eggs
350g/12oz/3 cups plain
   (all-purpose) flour
5ml/1 tsp baking powder
10ml/2 tsp vanilla sugar
fresh strawberries, to serve

For the filling and topping
3 gelatine leaves
1 litre/1¾ pints/4 cups double
   (heavy) cream
10ml/2 tsp sugar
10ml/2 tsp cornflour (cornstarch)
2 egg yolks
10ml/2 tsp vanilla sugar

For the marzipan
200g/7oz/1¾ cups ground almonds
200g/7oz/1¾ cups icing
   (confectioners') sugar
1 egg white
a few drops of green food colour

1 To make the marzipan, put the ground almonds in a bowl and add the icing sugar and egg white. Mix to form a paste.

2 Add a few drops of green food colour and knead until evenly coloured. Refrigerate in a plastic bag for up to 3 days until required.

3 Preheat the oven to 180°C/350°F/ Gas 4. Grease and line a 20cm/8in round cake tin (pan).

4 Put the butter and sugar in a large bowl and beat until fluffy. Add the eggs and whisk together. Sift in the flour, baking powder and vanilla sugar and stir together.

5 Spoon the batter into the cake tin and bake for 1 hour, or until firm to the touch. Leave to cool in the tin. When cold, slice in half horizontally.

6 To make the filling, soak the gelatine in cold water according to the directions on the packet. Put half of the cream, the sugar, cornflour and egg yolks in a pan and heat gently, stirring constantly, until the mixture thickens. Do not allow it to boil or the eggs will curdle.

7 Pour into a bowl, and stir in the soaked gelatine leaves. Leave to cool.

8 Put the remaining cream with the vanilla sugar in a bowl and whisk until stiff.

9 Fold into the cooled custard and quickly spread half the mixture over the bottom layer of cake. Put the other cake layer on top and spread the remaining custard over the top and sides.

10 Put the marzipan between two sheets of foil. Roll out a thin round. Remove the top sheet of foil and, using a 30cm/12in diameter plate as a guide, cut a marzipan circle.

11 Use the foil to lift the marzipan circle over the top of the cake and smooth it down the sides. Trim the edge around the cake base. Decorate with fresh strawberries.

Energy 1326kcal/5512kJ; Protein 11.3g; Carbohydrate 112g, of which sugars 77.6g; Fat 95.7g, of which saturates 56.1g; Cholesterol 346mg; Calcium 191mg; Fibre 1.9g; Sodium 218mg.

Croquembouche

This stunning tower is made from tiny, light-as-air choux buns filled with cream and delicately drizzled with caramel. Croquembouche is served in France for special occasions such as weddings and tastes wonderful. Be careful when you make the caramel, as it can easily burn.

SERVES 10

75g/3oz/6 tbsp unsalted butter,
  plus extra for greasing
115g/4oz/1 cup plain (all-purpose)
  flour, sifted
3 eggs

For the filling
600ml/1 pint/2¼ cups double
  (heavy) cream
60ml/4 tbsp caster (superfine) sugar

For the caramel
115g/4oz/generous ½ cup caster
  (superfine) sugar

1 Preheat the oven to 200°C/400°F/ Gas 6. Grease four baking sheets.

2 Melt the butter in a pan with 250ml/8fl oz/1 cup water and bring to the boil. Remove from the heat.

3 Sift the flour on to a paper sheet and immediately pour into the pan.

COOK'S TIP
Bake the buns a day ahead and store unfilled in an airtight box.

4 Quickly beat together until the mixture forms a ball.

5 Transfer to a bowl and whisk in the eggs, using an electric whisk, until a smooth, thick paste forms.

6 Fill a piping (pastry) bag fitted with a 1cm/½in plain nozzle and pipe small balls about 2.5cm/1in wide on to the baking sheets, spaced well apart.

COOK'S TIP
Freeze unfilled buns in a plastic box. Keep for 2 months. Thaw, then re-heat in the oven at 180°C/ 350°F/Gas 4 for 10 minutes. Cool, then fill as step 9.

7 Bake for 20 minutes, or until golden. Pierce a large hole in the base of each to release the steam, then return to the oven for a further 5 minutes. Cool on a wire rack.

8 To make the filling, whip the cream together with the 60ml/4 tbsp sugar, until it forms soft peaks.

9 Spoon into a piping bag fitted with a 5mm/¼in nozzle and pipe cream into each bun through the hole in the base.

10 Arrange the buns in a pyramid.

11 To make the caramel, slowly heat the sugar until liquid in a pan.

12 Drizzle the hot caramel over the pyramid, allowing it to drizzle down over the buns. Serve immediately.

Energy 579kcal/2400kJ; Protein 6g; Carbohydrate 32.6g, of which sugars 24.4g; Fat 46.8g, of which saturates 28.3g; Cholesterol 159mg; Calcium 123mg; Fibre 0.3g; Sodium 138mg.

Gâteau Saint Honoré

Named after the patron saint of bakers, this spectacular dessert has a puff pastry base topped with caramel-coated choux puffs and filled with crème pâtissière. The cake is then drizzled with threads of golden caramel. Make and eat this fresh for a special occasion; do not refrigerate.

SERVES 10

175g/6oz puff pastry, thawed
   if frozen
flour, for dusting

For the choux pastry
300ml/½ pint/1¼ cups water
115g/4oz/½ cup butter, diced
130g/4½oz/generous 1 cup plain
   (all-purpose) flour, sifted
pinch of salt
4 eggs, lightly beaten
beaten egg, to glaze

For the crème pâtissière
3 egg yolks
50g/2oz/¼ cup caster
   (superfine) sugar
30ml/2 tbsp plain
   (all-purpose) flour
30ml/2 tbsp cornflour (cornstarch)
300ml/½ pint/1¼ cups milk
150ml/¼ pint/⅔ cup double
   (heavy) cream
30ml/2 tbsp orange liqueur

For the caramel
225g/8oz/generous 1 cup sugar
120ml/4fl oz/½ cup water

1 Roll out the puff pastry on a lightly floured surface, and cut out a 20cm/8in circle using a flan ring or an upturned plate as your guide.

2 Put the pastry round on a baking sheet lined with baking parchment. Prick all over with a fork and chill while you make the choux pastry.

3 To make the choux pastry, put the water and butter in a large pan. Heat until the butter has melted, then bring to the boil.

4 Add the flour and salt to the pan in one go. Remove the pan from the heat and beat vigorously until the mixture leaves the sides of the pan.

5 Beat in the eggs, a little at a time, to form a glossy paste.

6 Preheat the oven to 200°C/400°F/Gas 6.

7 Spoon the choux pastry into a piping (pastry) bag fitted with a 1cm/½in plain nozzle. Pipe a spiral of choux on to the puff pastry base, starting at the edge and working toward the centre.

8 Use the remaining choux pastry to pipe 16 small buns, using the same plain nozzle, on to a lightly greased baking sheet. Brush the buns and the choux pastry spiral with egg to glaze.

9 Bake the small buns for about 20 minutes until golden, and bake the choux-topped puff pastry on the shelf below for 35 minutes, or until well risen.

Energy 466kcal/1952kJ; Protein 7.3g; Carbohydrate 51.9g, of which sugars 30.9g; Fat 26.5g, of which saturates 12.5g; Cholesterol 186mg; Calcium 139mg; Fibre 0.5g; Sodium 221mg.

10 Pierce several holes in the top and sides of the spiral, and pierce one small hole in the side of each bun, using a skewer. Return the pastry to the oven for 5 more minutes to dry out. Cool on a wire rack.

11 To make the crème pâtissière, whisk the egg yolks and caster sugar until light and creamy. Whisk in the flour and cornflour.

12 Bring the milk to the boil in a pan and pour over the egg mixture, whisking all the time. Return the custard to the cleaned pan and cook for 2–3 minutes, or until thickened and smooth. Remove from the heat, cover with dampened baking parchment and leave to cool.

13 Whip the cream lightly. Remove the paper from the crème pâtissière and fold in with the orange liqueur. Spoon half into a piping bag fitted with a small plain nozzle and use it to fill the choux buns.

14 To make the caramel, heat the sugar and water in a pan until dissolved, stirring occasionally. Bring to the boil and cook until it turns a rich golden colour. Remove the pan from the heat and set over a large bowl half-filled with boiling water to keep the caramel liquid.

15 Put the puff and choux pastry base on a serving plate.

16 Dip the bases of the choux buns into the caramel and arrange in a ring around the edge of the pastry.

17 Pipe the remaining crème pâtissière into the centre of the case. Drizzle the tops of the choux buns with the remaining caramel and leave to set. Keep in a cool place, but NOT the refrigerator, for up to 2 hours before serving.

Meringue mountain

A meringue can make a stunning centrepiece and is actually quite easy to make. Bake it ahead of time, if you like – it then takes just a few minutes to put together before serving. For best results bake the meringues slowly and leave them in the oven overnight to make them extra crisp.

SERVES 8–10

8 egg whites
450g/1lb/2 cups caster
 (superfine) sugar
pink food colouring
450ml/¾ pint/scant 2 cups double
 (heavy) cream
Materials: tiny rosebuds and
 candles, to decorate

1 Preheat the oven to 110°C/
225°F/Gas ½. Line three baking
sheets with baking parchment. Rinse
out a large, grease-free bowl with
boiling water, then dry completely.

2 Put the egg whites into the bowl
of an electric mixer. Whisk the
egg whites until they form soft
peaks. Whisk in the sugar, 15ml/
1 tbsp at a time, until the mixture
forms stiff peaks.

COOK'S TIPS
• Bake the meringues ahead and
store in an airtight tin in a dry
place for up to a week.
• This cake is not suitable
for freezing.

3 Remove a quarter of the mixture
and put it into a clean bowl. Colour
it a pale pink with food colouring.

4 Spoon the pink meringue
mixture into a piping (pastry) bag
fitted with a star nozzle and pipe
15 pink rosettes.

5 Spoon the remaining white
mixture into a piping bag fitted
with a star nozzle and pipe a thin
20cm/8in circle on to one of the
baking sheets. Pipe about 15
small white rosettes with the
remaining meringue.

6 Bake for 4 hours, swapping the
trays over in the oven halfway
through. Turn off the heat and
allow the meringues to dry out in
the oven overnight if possible.

7 To assemble, whip the cream until
it forms soft peaks, then spoon into
a piping bag.

8 Pipe a cone shape of cream on to
the circular base. Pipe a little cream
on the base of each meringue
rosette, then assemble them in a
conical shape.

9 Decorate with rosebuds and
candles, and serve immediately.

Energy 389kcal/1628kJ; Protein 3.3g; Carbohydrate 48.2g, of which sugars 48.2g; Fat 24.2g, of which saturates 13.5g; Cholesterol 59mg; Calcium 48mg; Fibre 0g; Sodium 68mg.

Index